LIBERTY
AND
LEARNING

LIBERTY
AND
LEARNING

The Evolution of American Education

LARRY P. ARNN
President, Hillsdale College

Hillsdale College Press, Hillsdale, Michigan
2004

HILLSDALE COLLEGE PRESS

Liberty and Learning: The Evolution of American Education

©2004 Hillsdale College Press, Hillsdale, Michigan 49242

First printing 2004

Printed in the United States of America

Printed and bound by Edwards Brothers, Ann Arbor, Michigan

Library of Congress Control Number 2004113006
ISBN 0-916308-00-6

To the faculty, staff, and students
of Hillsdale College

What spectacle can be more edifying or more season-
able, than that of Liberty and Learning, each leaning
on the other for their mutual and surest support?

—James Madison
letter to W. T. Barry
August 4, 1822

CONTENTS

❖ ❖ ❖

ACKNOWLEDGMENTS

❖ ❖ ❖

I OWE THANKS to many people who have assisted with the production of this book.

They begin with the staff in my office, the effective and tireless Pat Loper, Lisa Sprague, and Bethany Olson. Beth has chased down endless facts and documents, as she was well-trained to do here as a student at Hillsdale College.

My colleagues Will Morrissey, Robert Eden, and my old friends Tom West and Charles Kesler are all fine scholars, and they have taught me things and recommended things that are beneficial to this book.

I mentioned one of my teachers, Harry Jaffa, at length in the text. I must mention also Sir Martin Gilbert, now a colleague at Hillsdale College, whose standards of writing history are a privilege to witness and an impossibility to emulate.

Linda Moore, the College archivist, is capable, thorough, and devoted. She has found many of the best things in this book.

Both this book and my presence here at Hillsdale College were facilitated by the work of Arlan Gilbert, our College historian.

My friend and colleague of many years Douglas Jeffrey has edited better books than this, but he has benefited none of them more either in substance or style. His colleague and mine David Bobb did invaluable work making corrections and editorial suggestions. Eva Martin at the College and Christina Bych of aatec publications in Ann Arbor helped with copy-editing. Kim Tedders has been a shepherd of the work in Doug's office.

David Whalen told me important things that are written into the text.

Our eldest daughter Katy manifested her nature in helping to correct and edit this text. Her virtues, and those of her siblings Henry and Alice, reflect those of my wife of 25 years, dearest Penny. Of course my parents, Paul and the late and beloved Georgia, are the example that I follow whenever I do well.

I do all my work with and under a Board of Trustees. Our Chairman Emeritus Don Mossey said once that this board is the "seat of freedom in our country." This book shows that they have been so for a very long time. I am proud and grateful to work with the Chair, Bill Brodbeck; the Vice-Chair, Pat Sajak; and with the entire board.

INTRODUCTION
❖ ❖ ❖

THIS IS A STORY of three things and of how they are related. One is a particular college. One is the government under which it operates. The third is the education system of which it is a part. The story is told by comparing these things in three periods, three snapshots in time.

The college is Hillsdale College. The education system is in particular the colleges and universities of the United States, or what we in America call higher education. The government is the government of the United States.

Each of these three things has been subject to change. Both the government and the education system in the United States think that they have changed decisively because they had to change, because change is the essential way of things. Hillsdale College, on the other hand, understands itself in essentially the same way as it did at the beginning of its story. On this point, it has an important difference from both the government and the larger education system.

This difference is new. It was not present at the beginning. It is the source of controversy between Hillsdale College, on one hand, and the government and the education system, on the other.

Far from quarreling with the federal government at the beginning, Hillsdale College was among its strongest supporters, and this at its hour of most urgent need. The College had no aspirations for subsidy from it or from any government. It was not loyal to any government for its own sake, but as a means to an end. The end was the protection of our rights, especially our right to "civil and religious liberty" that the College names in the first sentence of its own founding document. Of course in the Civil War both sides claimed to be defending rights, and both sides claimed the authority of the Constitution for their actions. Hillsdale College sided with the cause of Union and constitutional abolition.[1]

Hillsdale College also had no quarrel at the beginning with other institutions of higher education. It was founded to pursue "liberal education." Its understanding of that term was not remarkably different from the understanding that prevailed from the time of the American Revolution until the College's founding in the middle of the nineteenth century. Liberal education was understood to carry certain crucial benefits for the regime of liberty, both for leading citizens and for the common life of republican government. It achieved these benefits through the study of old and permanent things, things higher than any fashion or policy, things for the sake of which all life is lived, if it is lived well.

Today Hillsdale College is still in the same place, still small, and still pursuing a curriculum essentially the same as in those first days. Meanwhile, both the education system and the government have changed. Hillsdale College is now at odds with most educational practices, just as it is at odds with most political practices. It was in the beginning a leader in a large and growing movement. Today it is a member of a tiny minority, a minority not quite but almost of one.

Hillsdale College claims that it has remained faithful to principles and practices that are true today, just as they were when it was built. It believes that if these principles and practices are not true today, then they were not true originally, when the College was founded. It believes that if they were true back at the beginning, then they must still be true today. It does not accept, then, the idea that truth changes with time.

The question whether truth changes with time has the most important consequences both for education and for government. Both kinds of consequences are easy to see. In education, it involves the character or quality of the thing being pursued. Is it the work of the scholar to seek, and the work of the teacher to impart, the nature or way or essence of

---

[1] There being no power in the original (unamended) Constitution to abolish slavery in the states, the proposal was to forbid its spread into the "Federal Territories," the land belonging to the United States not yet incorporated into the Union as states.

things, and in that to find their own purpose as scholars and as human beings? Or is it the work of the scholar to seek, and of the teacher to impart, the creative task of building a reality for his own time and a system of value to go with it?

In government it involves the status of the principles of right upon which our nation was built. The Declaration of Independence begins with the expression: "When in the course of human events. . . ." By this, it means to say that what follows is true for all time. When it goes on to mention "one people," it means to say that what follows is applicable to all people in all times and places. The idea of the "laws of nature and of nature's God" is another expression of this view.

In this question of the relationship among a college, a government, and the education system, the stakes are therefore high. They involve our understanding of the purpose of man, the nature of his rights, and the way he is to be governed.

1787

❖ ❖ ❖

In 1787, two documents were written that constitute the original understanding of education in America. Today it is not easy to recall those documents and what they mean. Their memory has been effaced by changes
of thought that accelerate still.

The great changes in education in the last half century have come in
the name of "Progress." Progress means that we know things today, and
have purposes today, that were unknown to the Founders of America.
According to this way of thinking, our knowledge and our purposes are
essentially different from those of the Founders. It follows from this that
the institutions the Founders set up when they built both our education
system and our government are obsolete, or at least insufficient.

An example can be found ready to hand in a current bill before the
United States Senate regarding the "reauthorization" of something called
the "Higher Education Act," originally passed in 1965. The bill is authored
by several leading senators, all of the same party. To avoid partisanship,
we will call this bill "The Party Bill." Later we will encounter two other
bills. They are sponsored by "The Other Party."

The Party Bill begins with certain "findings." The first of them is most
indicative, both of the nature of the bill and of the times in which we live.
This finding is that "a college education is more important than ever...."
This is true, the bill "finds," because there is more demand for college-
educated workers (due to a "shift in the economy") and because those
who have a college education make more money.

1

This assertion of the increased importance of education is useful not only to justify spending *more* money on it, but also to justify the spending of *any* money on it. The federal taxpayer has been spending money for education for a long time now, but still it is an innovation from the original idea of our Constitution. This innovation has been justified in considerable part by the discovery that education is more important than the Founders understood it to be. So says The Party Bill.

It being then a consequential point, we should raise the question: What did the American Founders understand to be the importance of education?

The authoritative statement regarding education from the period of the American founding is contained in the Northwest Ordinance of 1787. That document provides for the first time a way for a free government to control territory not properly part of its domain, and a way for that territory to join its domain by a regular procedure. It follows on the Land Ordinance of 1785 as the defining document for the control of the "Northwest Territory," which would eventually become the states of Michigan, Ohio, Illinois, Indiana, Wisconsin, and a portion of Minnesota. The Northwest Ordinance is still included as the third item in the United States Code. Alongside the Declaration of Independence, the Articles of Confederation, and the Constitution of United States, it is one of the four organic laws of the United States.

The third article of the Northwest Ordinance declares: "Religion, morality, and knowledge being necessary to good government and the happiness of mankind, schools and the means of education shall ever be encouraged."

Notice that these goods are said to be "necessary." This is a strong term. It means that without the one, there cannot be the other. Religion, morality, and knowledge are therefore essential for the highest reasons, reasons that transcend politics—that is why "happiness" is mentioned. But "good government" is mentioned, too. Both from the political point of view and from the higher point of view—both from the perspective of this world and of the next—"religion, morality, and knowledge" are indispensable.

Schools, furthermore, are means in service of "religion, morality, and knowledge," and therefore means also to "good government and the happiness of mankind." They are singled out here, the only means mentioned, although of course not the only ones existing. The mention of schools, and the failure to mention such things as families (which the Founders also saw as vital), indicates the priority given to education and also that it is a matter of special public interest.

As these high goods are said to depend upon "schools and the means of education," it makes sense that Congress would wish to encourage them. One would expect Congress to undertake something significant in this regard, and it did: In an earlier and connected fundamental law regarding the Federal Territories, the Land Ordinance of 1785, Congress had given a gift to education. It was a massive gift, a gift unprecedented and still unsurpassed. It is a gift not only of vast material meaning, but also a gift of priority.

The Land Ordinance of 1785 had provided a method for surveying and demarcating the Northwest Territory. It also indicated how the land would be disposed. Beginning at a point on the Pennsylvania border, the land was to be marked out in townships, each of which would contain 36 "sections," a section being one mile square. Of these 36 sections, four were to be reserved to the federal government for future sale and other purposes. Thirty-one were to be made available immediately for private purchase. And one, the 16th, was to be reserved "for the maintenance of public schools within the said Township."

The bulk of the land was therefore to be transferred to private hands immediately. This would be the rule through the passage of the great Homestead Act—signed into law by Abraham Lincoln in 1862—and it would continue into the twentieth century. In the beginning the government was keenly in search of money from these transactions. It was selling land to pay its debts. This changed with the Homestead Act, which gave the land away for the price of a filing fee and a commitment to live on the land and work it for five years.

These federal lands constituted one of the most precious resources ever held by any government. Most of what is now the United States was once simply an asset on the balance sheet of the federal government. The Civil War began in large part over a question of the administration of these lands—namely whether Congress had the power to exclude slavery from them. Their final settlement and incorporation as states marked an end to the beginning of our nation. As the New World had beckoned the first settlers to America, so the Western lands represented the promise of the nation. When George Washington named his army the "Continental Army," he was referring to this land, though no American would traverse the extent of the continent for more than a quarter of a century. That the bulk of it should be placed in the private sector immediately is a procla-mation of unmistakable meaning: The first priority when disposing of the greatest asset our government has ever held was that it become the prop-erty of individual citizens.

Consider in contrast how the deployment of land changed during the twentieth century. Look today at a map of the United States. Find one that shades in one color the parts held by the government, and in another the parts held privately. The farther east one looks, the larger the propor-tion of the land held privately; the farther west, the larger the proportion held by the government. That land in the west was settled later, as notions were changing about the relation between the individual and the govern-ment. This fact speaks volumes about the basic intention of the govern-ment in its first days and how it has changed in these latter days.[1]

Similarly the reservation of a section of the land within each township for a public purpose—a single public purpose placed above all others—ascribes by deed the same precedence expressed in word in the Northwest Ordinance.[2] The fact, the manner, and the justification of this gift elucidate the Founders' understanding of both government and education.

The manner of the gift is a piece of genius. This vast public resource is reserved in each township for education "in that township." This devo-

---

[1] U.S. General Services Administration Office of Governmentwide Policy, "Federal Real Property Profile: Overview of the United States Government's Owned and Leased Real Property as of September 30, 2003" (Washington, D.C., 2004), 16–17. This document shows that the federal government owns 66.7% of Alaska and 3.7% of Alabama; 46.9% of California and 11.8% of Arkansas; 50.2% of Arizona and 0.5% of Connecticut; 91.9% of Nevada and 6.2% of Georgia; and 49.7% of Oregon and 2.1% of Massachusetts.

[2] There is also a reservation of land in the Act to fulfill a previous commitment made to "soldiers of the late Continental Army."

tion of a nationally controlled asset to the benefit of its specific locality is one of the signal operations of federalism in our history. Schools and the means of education are to be encouraged as a national purpose. But they are to be encouraged through the agency and under the control of local hands. The Northwest Ordinance passed in what would prove to be the waning days of the Articles of Confederation, under which the central government was weak in dealing with localities. We will see below if that changes when a much stronger federal government is built under the new Constitution.

The justification for the gift would be given two years later in the Northwest Ordinance, in the passage we have already mentioned: "religion, morality, and knowledge being necessary to good government and the happiness of mankind, schools and the means of education shall ever be encouraged." This provides not only the justification for the gift, but also the purpose of the schools. If they are to be useful to good government and the happiness of mankind, they must be conducive to "religion, morality, and knowledge."

We think differently about the purposes of education today, to say the least. Prayer is now banned in public schools. Morality, when it is taught, is conceived as a subjective thing, or yet more commonly as a newly invented thing to be found under the heading "political correctness." The ideas of "knowledge," "good government," and "happiness" are now subjected to the tender care of deconstruction and historicism.

But regardless how much we think differently today about the purpose of education and its relation to "religion, morality, and knowledge," the Founders agree with us about one thing: They agree that education is *important*. It is fair to say indeed that the Founders regarded education to be of the utmost importance. They say so in the plainest language, and they say it in the most prominent of places. Moreover they support it by a gift so magnificent as to be beyond our power to emulate. By deed as much as by word, by example as much as by precept, they testify to the importance of education.

The Party Bill, then, is not at its best when it is teaching us history.

Notice the difference in emphasis between The Party Bill and the Northwest Ordinance. In this modern legislation, education is important for material reasons: People can make more money if they get a college degree. The subjects in question are not students, but consumers. In other places in The Party Bill people appear not only as consumers, but also as members of a race. The Party Bill is very concerned that people of one color more commonly go to college, or are more apt to go to graduate school and become teachers, than people of another color. Material conditions such as wealth and race dominate—indeed to the exclusion of all else—this modern piece of legislation.

The Northwest Ordinance supplied material means—the 16th section of each township—for purposes that rise above the material. In the Northwest Ordinance, the human being is seen as capable of elevation in the true sense. In his relation to God and his potential for happiness through the acquisition of knowledge and morality, the human being rises above matter to partake of the divine.

It is true that the Founders of America began their revolution in part on a question of taxation, a material question. Such things are important in and of themselves, but for the Founders they are important even more because they involve these higher elements. The Declaration of Independence ends with a pledge by its authors "to each other." They pledge their "fortunes, lives, and sacred honor" in support of the Declaration. The Declaration performs an act: the declaring of independence from Great Britain. This act is justified as a "good" thing, a moral thing. It is justified under the "laws of nature and of nature's god." It is justified by the "self-evident truth" that all men are created equal.

These ultimate questions involved in the American Revolution—questions that involve the ideas most important to the Founders—are of course the subject matter of a certain kind of education. They are specifically the questions raised and investigated in the pursuit of a "liberal education." The Northwest Ordinance is a document that takes the perspective of the "liberal arts." In contrast, The Party Bill is at best merely technical. At worst it reduces the human being to the material needs he has in common with every animal.

The Party Bill, it must be admitted, does reflect one part of the truth about education. Education is chiefly for the young, and it is time-consuming. It is mainly what young people do in preparation for, and before they begin living, their adult lives. Because it comes early, and because it is time-consuming, education is not compatible with the work of making a living, at least not full-time. Thus resources must be provided from some source if the young are to accomplish the task successfully.

If this is a natural phenomenon, and if education is important, one wonders then why the Founders would not wish to support education directly, in the same way that The Party Bill does. Indeed one wonders why they would not support it as the top priority, if it is so terribly important to such high and vital things. The answer to this question is to be found in Philadelphia in the summer of 1787.

The Northwest Ordinance was passed by Congress on July 13, 1787, in New York City. Beginning on May 14, and continuing until September 17 of the same summer, another body was meeting in Philadelphia. It met to amend the Articles of Confederation under which the Northwest Ordinance was passed. In fact it set quickly about the job of drafting a new document that would eventually become the Constitution.

The Articles of Confederation and the Constitution differ drastically in the power given to the central government. Under the Articles there was, for example, no federal power to tax individual citizens directly or to coin money. States could impose their own duties and imposts on foreign goods. Voting in the Congress was by state, and it took nine votes—more than two-thirds—to pass most things. Amendment of the articles required unanimity.

Under the Articles, states were not always careful with the rights of their citizens or of the interests of the Union. Rhode Island devalued its currency and forced creditors to accept that currency in payment of debts, in effect expropriating assets from some for the benefit of others. States passed tariffs on each other's goods and held negotiations of their own with European powers, particularly the British. The Union could do nothing to prevent these abuses of rights at home or to maintain a strong and united front to the world.

Concerned about this, those who called the Constitutional Convention intended to make a much stronger central government. The arguments for and against this, especially as they are found in The Federalist and in Anti-Federalist responses, are classics of political argument worthy of any age. The plan that was reached in the Convention went far short of a complete centralizing of government. Probably no one had aimed for this in any case, although the supporters of the Constitution were accused of it.

Hamilton did move in the Convention that the federal government be granted "power to pass all laws whatsoever."[3] Serving on Washington's staff during the Revolutionary War, Hamilton had struggled, along with Washington, to get the Army paid from a Congress that had neither funds nor means to get them. He had watched generals appeal around George Washington directly to Congress, the many-headed beast, for advancement.[4] He was concerned when, after the war, states interrupted trade, devalued debts, and inflated their currencies.

This broad suggestion by Hamilton for the scope of federal power found little support in the Convention. There were two reasons for this. The obvious one was the jealousy, or perhaps justified suspicion, of the states. They had banded together to fight against a despotic central power, and now they enjoyed great power of their own. Both conviction and interest suggested they should not give it up. But these thoughts are related to a higher and a positive reason, a reason central to the idea of constitutionalism as it was born in America.

Like separation of powers, federalism is a method for the division of power, both to prevent tyranny and to increase the chance of good government. It grew in part from the historical accident that the colonies were established and developed independently, that their dispute with the mother country proceeded for a time at different rates, and that they came together in steps or stages leading up to the Declaration of Independence. It

---

[3] Legislative enactments, in Hamilton's plan, were subject to executive veto. See Madison's account of Hamilton's June 18, 1787, speech at the Constitutional Convention in Madison, Notes of Debates in the Federal Convention of 1787 (New York: W. W. Norton, 1987), 138.

[4] See Hamilton's letter to James Duane of September 3, 1780, in which he writes about the Confederacy that, "The fundamental defect is the want of power in the Congress." Harold C. Syrett, ed., The Papers of Alexander Hamilton, Vol. II (New York: Columbia University Press, 1961), 401. For wrangling over funding with Congress, and the insubordination of members of the Army, see the fine book by Richard Brookhiser, Alexander Hamilton, American (New York: Simon & Schuster, 1999), 54.

grew also from the thinking that power must be divided in ways that permit its vigorous use but protect against abuse. The states, which were stronger than the central government under the Articles, inherited English common law police power. This gave them the authority to legislate "in all cases whatsoever" for the "health, safety, and general welfare of the people." A stronger federal government, divided into branches and possessed of wide but enumerated powers, could restrain the power of states and diversify the places where authority is exercised.[5]

James Madison, the "Father of the Constitution," describes this division of labor with his usual clarity in *Federalist* 45:

> The powers delegated by the proposed Constitution to the federal Government, are few and defined. Those which are to remain in the State governments are numerous and indefinite. The former will be exercised principally on external objects, as war, peace, negotiation, and foreign commerce; with which last the power of taxation will, for the most part, be connected. The powers reserved to the several States will extend to all the objects which, in the ordinary course of affairs, concern the lives, liberties, and properties of the people; and the internal order, improvement, and prosperity of the State.[6]

---

[5] It is true that Madison, like many of the Founders, had more than one opinion on what should be the precise division of authority between the states and the federal government. He wrote to Washington on April 16, 1787: "Conceiving that an individual independence of the States is utterly irreconcilable with their aggregate sovereignty; and that a consolidation of the whole into one simple republic would be as inexpedient as it is unattainable, I have sought for some middle ground, which may at once support a due supremacy of the national authority, and not exclude the local authorities wherever they can be subordinately useful." James Madison, *The Papers of James Madison*, William M. E. Rachal, ed., vol. 9 (Chicago: University of Chicago Press, 1975), 383. Later in the same letter Madison favors a veto by the federal government of all legislative acts by the states. The final agreement reached in Philadelphia and through the state ratifying conventions was the product of no one of the Founders alone, but of all of them together. The system that was developed kept substantial powers—almost complete powers over local matters—in the states.

[6] Alexander Hamilton, James Madison, and John Jay, *The Federalist Papers*, ed. Clinton Rossiter, with an introduction and notes by Charles R. Kesler (New York: Mentor, 2003), 289.

One cannot help emphasizing here that "the powers reserved to the several States will extend to all the objects, which, in the ordinary course of affairs, concern the lives, liberties, and properties of the people; and the internal order, improvement, and prosperity of the State." Education is of course a prime example of the kind of thing reserved to the states.

The authors of the Constitution had deep reasons for organizing power as they did. Above all, their purpose was to achieve a government of majority rule that would protect the rights of all. They understood that aristocracy or monarchy on the one hand, and democracy on the other, had been consistently ineffective at this in the past. Rare indeed—or rather nonexistent—was the government that operated from generation to generation according to the popular will and protecting the rights of majority and minority alike.

The men meeting in Philadelphia in 1787 thought they understood the reason for this problem. Several passages in the The Federalist, for example, form a commentary upon or an elaboration of the key doctrines of the Declaration of Independence. In particular they addressed the question of what it means to declare, under the authority of the "laws of nature and of nature's God," that "all men are created equal, and endowed by their Creator with certain unalienable rights."

Madison provides a key to understanding equality in Federalist 51:

> But what is government itself but the greatest of all reflections on human nature? If men were angels, no government would be necessary. If angels were to govern men, neither external nor internal controls on government would be necessary. In framing a government which is to be administered by men over men, the great difficulty lies in this: you must first enable the government to control the governed; and in the next place oblige it to control itself.[7]

---

[7] Ibid., 319.

This is in the first place a piece of plain good sense. Anyone who has been to a committee meeting knows that people are not angels. Especially acting in committees, they are not to be trusted with arbitrary power. But more than a piece of good sense only, this passage is a statement on human nature and, specifically, on the sense in which each human being is "created equal." It is in comparison to other creatures that the meaning of human equality becomes clear.[8]

By mention of angels, Madison contrasts the nature of the human being with the divine. His friend Jefferson mentioned God four times in the Declaration of Independence, once as each of the three types of rule.[9] As the maker of the laws of nature and of nature's God, He is the legislator. As the Supreme Judge of the World, He is the judge. As the protector, Divine Providence, He is the executive. In His hands alone are all the powers of government to be concentrated. God and his angels, say the authors of the Declaration and the Constitution, can be trusted in ways that humans cannot.

As the angels are above us, below us are the beasts. At the end of his life Thomas Jefferson was invited, along with the still-living John Adams, to attend ceremonies marking the fiftieth anniversary of the Declaration. These ceremonies were to be held in Washington. Both men were too ill to attend, and indeed both of them would die on the very day of the celebration. In responding with regret to the invitation, Jefferson wrote to Roger Weightman about the meaning of the document.

> All eyes are opened, or opening, to the rights of man. The general spread of the light of science has already laid open to every

---

[8] In the *Politics*, Aristotle writes of political life, "One who is incapable of participating or who is in need of nothing through being self-sufficient is no part of a city, and so is either a beast or a god." Aristotle, *Politics* 1253 a 28–29, trans. Carnes Lord (Chicago: University of Chicago Press, 1984), 37. On this important idea, and its relationship to equality, Harry V. Jaffa has written much. See Jaffa, *A New Birth of Freedom: Abraham Lincoln and the Coming of the Civil War* (Lanham, MD: Rowman & Littlefield, 2000), 167. Also see Jaffa, "Equality as a Conservative Principle," in *How To Think About the American Revolution: A Bicentennial Cerebration* (Claremont, CA: Claremont Institute, 2001), 41–42.

[9] George Anastaplo first made this observation about the Declaration's references to God and their relationship to the separation of powers. See Anastaplo, *The Constitution of 1787: A Commentary* (Baltimore, MD: Johns Hopkins University Press, 1989), 21.

view the palpable truth, that the mass of mankind has not been born with saddles on their backs, nor a favored few booted and spurred, ready to ride them legitimately, by the grace of God.[10]

If men are not angels, neither are they beasts. They have a special nature, which requires a form of government proper to them, and different from the form proper to angels and to beasts. According to the Founders, it is in this special nature that one finds both the need for government and the need for government to be limited.

This understanding of human nature also carries implications for the purpose of the governing structure of education. Liberal education is the study of ends—of the things for the sake of which choices are made and lives are lived. The Founders in their political understanding point up toward the permanent, the final, and the divine, in the same way that liberal education does. On the other hand, they do not give specific instructions for education in the way that the most famous of the classical founders did. Lycurgos, for example, prescribed precisely how Spartan children, especially the males, were to be taught. Although the Founders of America have a view of man that does imply an approach to education, they do not seek to control the administration of it.

The Founders did not seek administrative control of education because the nature of man is, in their view, best able to flourish under a regime of limited government. And if the government is to be limited, then control of even vital things like education must be decentralized. The elevation of their view of the human being limits the dictates they give in every subject, including education.

In our constitutional system many vital things are specifically excluded from federal control, and many other vital things are excluded from any form of government control whatsoever. Property is to be in private hands, and therefore food is to be grown on private farms. Churches are to be run by private people, attended by those who are willing to go. Children are to be conceived and raised by private people, who join in families

---

[10]Thomas Jefferson, letter to Roger Weightman (June 24, 1826), *The Writings of Thomas Jefferson*, vol. XV, ed. Albert E. Bergh (Washington, D.C.: Thomas Jefferson Memorial Association, 1904), 182.

for the purpose, and when they decide to do it. These things are matters of the first importance. Some of them are vital to the simple functioning of society and the survival of its members. None of them are subjected to federal control.

In constitutional terms, this idea is enshrined in the principle of enumeration. Article 1, Section 8 of the Constitution contains 17 clauses that give specific grants of policy authority to the Congress. Of course, the 18th contains the statement that the Congress may do all things "necessary and proper" to achieve the first 17. Some of the Founders took an expansive view of this. Some took a restrictive view. None thought that the "necessary and proper" clause was or should have been a new grant of power that would permit Congress to do whatever it wished.[11]

Education, mark the point, is not mentioned in Article I, Section 8. Recall that the Northwest Ordinance was passed by the Confederation Congress in the very summer of 1787 in New York City that the Framers were meeting in Philadelphia to write the Constitution. It was the big political news of that summer that the Ordinance had been passed. Part of that big political news was the mention of education in the third article of the Ordinance. It is not possible that education was omitted by oversight from the Constitution.

We have seen that the Founders considered education to be of a massive importance, of the highest importance. We have seen that they found ways to subsidize it on a huge scale, but ways that preserved the ability of people engaged in education—ultimately parents, students, and teachers—to manage it themselves. They did this for reasons having to do strictly with education itself. They did it also for the sake of the central reasons behind the American Revolution.

There were several proposals for the support of education in a more direct way at the time of the founding. George Washington, the "Father of our

---

[11] Randy E. Barnett, "The Original Meaning of the Necessary and Proper Clause," *University of Pennsylvania Journal of Constitutional Law* 6 (2003): 183–220

Country" and the chairman of the Constitutional Convention, was among the chief proponents of a military academy, which was eventually established at West Point. He was also a strong proponent of education generally, including the establishment of a national university. As our first president, Washington gave "annual messages" as required in Article II, Section 3 of the Constitution—now known as "State of the Union" messages. His were very different, especially in their brevity, from State of the Union messages today. They seldom strayed from topics of direct and immediate concern of the executive administration or of legislative deliberation. In those days, such topics were few, generally fewer than ten items per speech. Among these few, education recurs.

In his first annual message, Washington stated the common view of the Founders that: "Knowledge is in every Country the surest basis of public happiness. In one, in which the measures of Government receive their impression so immediately from the sense of the Community as in ours, it is proportionably essential."[12] But he goes on to recommend that Congress promote this knowledge. In a passage that definitely foresaw the possibility of direct federal aid to colleges, he stated:

> Whether this desirable object will be best promoted by affording aids to Seminaries of Learning already established—by the institution of a national University—or by any other expedients, will be well worthy of a place in the deliberations of the Legislature.[13]

The national university has never been built, and federal aid to "seminaries of learning" would not come to be for more than 150 years. Washington himself took no detailed position on the constitutionality of either proposal. The Founders conducted an extensive discussion of the national university, and its constitutionality was an issue debated by several of them.

Washington pushed the idea of a national university with all his might. He mentioned it several times in his annual messages and in let-

---

[12] George Washington, "[First Annual Message] To the United States Senate and House of Representatives," (Jan. 8, 1790), W. W. Abbot, ed., *The Papers of George Washington, Presidential Series*, vol. 4 (Charlottesville: University Press of Virginia, 1993), 545.

[13] Ibid.

ters to colleagues in the government. In his will he left a bequest of 50 shares of the Potomac Company "towards the endowment of a University to be established within the limits of the District of Columbia, under the auspices of the general government, if that government should incline to extend a fostering hand towards it."[14] Attempts to establish this university would continue for more than 100 years. These attempts ran afoul of concerns about the cost—such concerns being much more common early in our history than in recent years. But there was also a constitutional concern, and it was serious.

The Eleventh Congress, meeting in February 1811, referred to committee a suggestion by President Madison that they consider "the establishment of a seminary of learning by the national legislature." Madison explained the idea:

> Whilst it is universally admitted that a well instructed people alone, can be permanently a free people; and whilst it is evident that the means of diffusing and improving useful knowledge, form so small a proportion of the expenditures for national purposes, I cannot presume it to be unseasonable, to invite your attention to the advantages of superadding, to the means of Education provided by the several States, a Seminary of Learning instituted by the national Legislature, within the limits of their exclusive jurisdiction; the expense of which might be defrayed, or reimbursed, out of the vacant grounds which have accrued to the Nation within those limits.[15]

Thus under the guiding hand of Madison, the idea of support for "seminaries of learning" was restricted to one national university, located within the limits of the District of Columbia. Funds for the university were to be provided by the sale of vacant lands within the confines of the Dis-

---

[14] George Washington, "Last Will and Testament," (July 9, 1799), W. W. Abbot, ed., *The Papers of George Washington, Retirement Series*, vol. 4 (Charlottesville: University Press of Virginia, 1999), 483.

[15] James Madison, "Annual Message to Congress" (December 5, 1810), J. C. A. Stagg, ed., *The Papers of James Madison, Presidential Series*, vol. 3 (Charlottesville: University Press of Virginia, 1996), 52.

trict. Of course Madison had as much authority as any man to speak on the constitutionality of any proposal, and here he is speaking as president of the United States to a friendly legislature. This makes the response he got all the more surprising.

New York Congressman Samuel L. Mitchill, who with President Madison was a Republican, was the chairman of the reporting committee at the time. Mitchill began his response by agreeing that the national university was a splendid idea. Anyway, he admitted that it was endorsed by "authorities so respectable" as to carry great weight. He then raised a problem, however:

> [I]t was necessary to consider whether Congress possessed the power to found and endow a national university. It is argued, from the total silence of the Constitution, that such a power has not been granted to Congress, inasmuch as the only means by which it is therein contemplated to promote the progress of science and the useful arts is, by securing to authors and inventors exclusive right to their respective writings and discoveries for limited times. The Constitution, therefore, does not warrant the creation of such corporation by any express provision.[16]

Mitchill and the committee went on to admit that the land of the District of Columbia was wholly within the power of the Congress, thus that they might be able to devote some of it to the purpose of a university. Still, the problem persisted that "the endowment of a university is not ranked among the objects for which drafts are to be made upon the treasury. The money of the nation seems to be reserved for other uses."[17]

The contemporary reader will likely not be quick to grasp what has happened here. George Washington and James Madison, each in his capacity as president, asked the Congress for something. The one is the chairman of the convention that adopted the Constitution; the other is its

---

[16] House Select Committee, "which relates to the establishment of a seminary of learning by the National Legislature," Report to the House of Representatives, read by Rep. Samuel L. Mitchill (Republican–NY), February 18, 1811, 11th Cong., 3d sess., 1811, *Annals of Congress*, 976.

[17] Ibid.

principal author. And the Congress replies that the document neither justifies nor empowers them to accede to the request.

Admittedly, the view of Mitchill's committee was not quite the uniform view. In 1816, under the presidency of James Monroe, another committee recommended to Congress the expenditure of some $200,000 for the purpose of building a national university. This money, too, was to be raised by selling vacant land within the District of Columbia. The committee recommended that action because "the means are ample, the end desirable, the object fairly within the legislative powers of Congress...."[18] The bill was "indefinitely postponed" on the floor of the House in March of 1817.[19]

Even if some thought that land could be sold and the proceeds used for education, that is a far cry from direct taxation to support it, and further yet from the system of detailed federal regulation that now persists. Scruples about the extent of power granted to the federal government were very common in the first decades of American history. Today, by contrast, such scruples are almost nonexistent. Entire presidential campaigns take place with hardly a mention of the Constitution, and generally none about any restriction it might place on federal government action. Thus the fact that education has in recent decades become a matter of federal government administrative control is hardly considered controversial. There is not even a memory that such issues were once—not even that long ago—a matter of serious debate.

One might say that it is because the Founders possessed a liberal education that they knew better than to make education an administrative fiefdom of a central power. It is the loss of that education among powerful people today that works to deny it to others. How did that loss occur? To find the answer to that we must move forward into the next century.

---

[18] House Select Committee, "to whom was referred so much of the President's Message as relates to the subject of a National University," Report to the House of Representatives, December 11, 1816, 14th Cong., 2d sess., 1816, *Annals of Congress*, 259.

[19] March 3, 1817, 14th Cong., 2d sess., 1817, *Annals of Congress*, 1064.

1844

❖ ❖ ❖

HILLSDALE COLLEGE was founded in 1844, a little nearer in time—and vastly nearer in thought—to the American founding than to the current day. Even as it was being established, seeds of change were being sown elsewhere in the country. These would sprout into an entirely different educational system than the one proceeding from the Northwest Ordinance and the Constitution. In the nineteenth century, then, we have two stories to tell. One provides an example of what was intended by the Founders. The other uncovers the roots of the system we have today. The contrast between them is stark.

Let us first consider what was intended: Hillsdale College began small and poor. It was built originally in Spring Arbor, Michigan, 30 miles up the road from its current location, and was called Michigan Central College. Its founders were mainly from western New York and New England. Several were preachers. All were devout. The first words the College proclaimed recall the themes of the Northwest Ordinance:

> Whereas the denomination of Christians, known as free-will Baptist, with other friends of education, grateful to God for the inestimable blessings resulting from the prevalence of civil and religious liberty and intelligent piety in the land, and believing that the diffusion of sound learning is essential to the perpetuity of these blessings, have founded and endowed a college. . . .[1]

---

[1] These Articles of Association were filed with the Michigan legislature in 1855, the eleventh year of the College's operation.

This quote is from the preamble to the Articles of Association of Hillsdale College, which were accepted by the State of Michigan eleven years after the College began operation. This delay resulted from a law passed in the State Legislature that prohibited the incorporation of new colleges in order to protect the University of Michigan. Obstruction from the government came early in the history of Hillsdale College.

The founding of Hillsdale was singular in another respect. The Articles of Association speak of the "diffusion" of sound learning. They meant this broadly and seriously. The Articles promise to offer to "all persons who wish, irrespective of nationality, color, or sex," a "literary, scientific, or theological education." Hillsdale College is, we believe, the first institution of higher learning founded, anywhere in the world, with an expressed commitment to accept black and white, man and woman, impartially. It is, so far as we can tell, the third actually to do it. In accordance with this commitment to the "diffusion" of sound learning, the College made vigorous efforts from the beginning to keep costs low and to find support from private sources to enable any qualified student to attend the College.

After nine years in Spring Arbor, several college leaders formed the view that the College should move to a larger town—in part to find more funds for the support of the students. In 1853 they chose Hillsdale. Hillsdale was at the time a tiny village of only 2,000 (today only 10,000), but it was located along the railway, which gave it the communications of a metropolis.

The decision to move to Hillsdale was influenced also by an accident of personality. The representative of the College to the town of Hillsdale was Ransom Dunn. A man of immense energy and determination, of fierce conviction and eloquence, of profound reflection and faith, Dunn would work for the College for 50 years, until the dawn of the twentieth century. One of his favorite sayings was that "the moment we fold our arms and cease to make aggressive movements, we die."[2] It was no weak man who rode his horse into Hillsdale on the cold evening of January 14, 1853. It was no weak partnership that he would form there.

Dunn stopped at the larger of two local hotels and asked that the town leaders be gathered to discuss education. Several came. They met

---

[2] Arlan K. Gilbert, *Ransom Dunn*. Forthcoming from Hillsdale College Press.

first in the pharmacy, then adjourned to the courthouse. Dunn stated the purposes of the College: "One thing must be distinctly understood: that the school from the first is to be a denominational one but not sectarian, furnishing no special advantages to any denomination, nor refusing favor to any; neither does it propose to make distinctions on the ground of sex or color."[3] Soon the town and the College agreed together to raise $15,000 each for construction of a new facility to be called Hillsdale College.

A total capitalization of $30,000 was no small sum in those days. Quickly the town exceeded its goal, and this put pressure on the College. Dunn—along with Edmund Fairfield, the key leader in the effort—undertook to raise $10,000 from the territory west of the Great Lakes. He moved his family to Wisconsin and traveled the area month after month, from town to town and from farm to farm. He talked to individuals. He preached at church services. He asked whoever he met to give whatever they could. Receiving gifts of a dollar or two at a time, or $5 or $10 from the more generous or affluent, he raised money for 18 months. He came back with $22,000. His report upon the campaign has the spirit of Caesar's upon his victory in Asia Minor:[4] "Was sent after $10,000. *Secured.*"[5]

It is worth asking what the farmers and tradesmen of Michigan, Wisconsin, and elsewhere expected for the money they gave. Dunn did not promise that the students or faculty would give the farmers advice about agriculture or the tradesmen about trade. Nor did he promise that the students would become better farmers or tradesmen themselves. The goods he offered were to be found in the character and minds of the students and in their disposition toward things that Americans love. Of course this was not a direct good to the farmers themselves. Indeed, they were giving so that others unknown to them could have advantages that they themselves would never enjoy. This made them servants, not so much of the students and faculty, but of what the students and faculty would learn and teach. In that sense they were partners with those in the College who would do the work. The cause stated in the preamble to the College's Arti-

---

[3] Arlan K. Gilbert, *Historic Hillsdale College: Pioneer in Higher Education*, 1844–1900 (Hillsdale, MI: Hillsdale College Press, 1991), 28.

[4] Julius Caesar wrote: "*Veni, vidi, vici*" ("I came, I saw, I conquered").

[5] Arlan K. Gilbert, *Historic Hillsdale College*, 36–37.

cles of Association—the cause of "civil and religious liberty and intelligent piety"—requires the service of many and offers many ways of serving.

The College was not then, nor is it now, in any sense what we today would call a policy shop. Its earliest catalog describes the curriculum for the 1845–1846 academic year. It was divided into the Preparatory Department and the Collegiate Department. The preparatory courses included English grammar, geography, arithmetic, Latin grammar, Sallust, Cicero, Virgil, Greek grammar and reader, the Gospels, and weekly declamations. The College department curriculum included algebra, geometry, trigonometry, Livy, Virgil, writing in Latin and Greek, physiology, and history. The sophomore level introduced Cicero, Demosthenes, *The Iliad*, logic, rhetoric, botany, and more writing of Latin and Greek. Later came chemistry, astronomy, philosophy, Tacitus, and Hebrew or French. In 1849, a significant new course was introduced: "The Constitution of the United States, Constitution of England, and Constitution of Man." By the late 1850s this course had been truncated to "The Constitution of the United States." In this context it is worth noting that beginning with the freshmen who will enter Hillsdale College in August 2004, each student will be required to take a full-semester course titled "The Constitution of the United States."[6] Historian David McCullough has recently remarked that there are but three institutions of higher learning in the nation that require such a course: the three service academies.[7] Now they are joined by a fourth.

One may wonder why, with such devotion to the ideas and purposes of America, the curriculum would not focus on its history and institutions more tightly. Most of it did not. The answer lies in the character of sound learning itself. Liberal education is the kind that deals not so much with means as with ends, not so much with the how of things as with the why.[8] In one sense this is irrelevant to the everyday pressures of life and especially the hard job of making a living. The doctor must know the body and

---

[6] The course syllabus is available from Hillsdale College. Also available is the course reading packet of primary source documents, prepared by the Hillsdale College political science faculty members who teach it.

[7] Congress, Senate, Committee on Health, Education, Labor, and Pensions, David McCullough, "Putting the Teaching of American History and Civics Back in the Classroom," 108th Cong., 1st sess., 10 April 2003, 13.

its workings; does he need to know its purposes? The accountant must know the ways of financial transactions and how to keep track of them; does he need to know the purpose of the business, or the best uses of the profits that it generates? The general needs to know how to assemble, supply, transport, and deploy his troops so as to defeat the enemy; does he need to know if the cause of his country is superior to the cause of the enemy? Are these people in fact experts in the ultimate questions that are inherent in their activities, and would they be better at these activities if they were?

The answer to this question given by the College in its first days is yes. Every self-governing person—every mother and father, every manager of a task or of other people—will find himself involved during his life with important decisions that reach up to the ultimate. Each must account to his Maker. Each must raise his children and answer their questions. Each must choose his field of labor and decide how honestly, diligently, and fairly he will pursue it. Each will face occasions when his own immediate interest conflicts with that of another, and each must decide then how far to pursue it or when to surrender that interest. The ability to do so is a product of liberal, as opposed to simply technical, education.

"Civil and religious liberty" are named as one of the two beneficiaries of "sound learning" in the Hillsdale Articles of Association. These are also the highest principles of the nation. In other words, the purposes of education are political as well as academic. The curriculum of Hillsdale College invites the student—nay, promises the student that he will be taught—to understand these purposes in light of the highest human ends. This is especially vital in America because in a free society governed by consent, each person is both governed and governor. Each must then practice the art of the statesman to some extent.

Writing of the classical authors Pythagoras, Plato, and Aristotle, Bishop Berkeley said famously: "And, whatever the world may say, he who hath not

---

[8] Hillsdale College faculty members Drs. David Whalen (English) and Mark Kalthoff (History) teach a course titled "*Artes Liberales*: The History and Literature of Liberal Education" that explores this subject extensively and well. The syllabus is available from Hillsdale College. See also Dr. Michael Bauman, "The Second Death of Socrates" (http://www.boundless.org/features/a0000913.html)

much meditated upon God, the human mind, and the *summum bonum*, may possibly make a thriving earthworm, but will most indubitably make a sorry patriot and a sorry statesman."[9] Related to this, the elder Thomas Jefferson wrote a letter to Henry Lee about the sources of the Declaration of Independence. He identified these sources as the "harmonizing sentiments of the day." These harmonizing sentiments, he says, are to be found in "conversation, in letters, in printed essays, or in the elementary books of public right, as Aristotle, Cicero, Locke, Sidney, &c."[10] Thus the discussion of ordinary citizens, if properly instructed, reflects and reveals the "laws of nature and of nature's God" that distinguish good action from bad, justice from injustice, liberty from license, and freedom from tyranny. This, too, is the promise of liberal education.

Among the people who devised, taught, and implemented the early curriculum at Hillsdale College was Edmund Fairfield, the second president of the College, who would later become lieutenant governor of Michigan and one of the founders of the Republican Party. Fairfield gave a speech upon the laying of the cornerstone of the new college building at Hillsdale on July 4, 1853. Titled "The College and the Republic," this speech makes plain why liberal education is important to liberty.[11]

The history of liberty, Fairfield said, is the history of intelligence. Ignorance is prerequisite to slavery: the more ignorance, the more slavery. The purpose of the College will be the cultivation of character and mind. The student will be taught to see the whole human being. He will be reminded of the sentiment of Webster: "[T]he greatest thought of my life is that of my individual responsibility to God." A man who knows this, said Fairfield, is "forever above that level where the tyrant may find a facile subject."

---

[9] George Berkeley, *Siris* (London: 1744), 350.

[10] Thomas Jefferson, to Henry Lee (May 8, 1825), *The Writings of Thomas Jefferson*, vol. XV, 118–19.

[11] The full text of this speech is in Appendix III.

Fairfield explained why education must be diffused. In any nation, the "heir of sovereignty must be qualified to meet the responsibilities of kingly office. In a Republic the people are the kings." Those he addressed at this Independence Day ceremony were not "merely" lawmakers, but "make those that are lawmakers." They lack the insignia of aristocratic nobility "in the shape of ribbons, red and green and blue." They have instead the insignia of "nature's nobility," which are "the hand hardened by toil, the face radiant with intelligence and manly virtue."

Fairfield's speech finds an echo in one of the finest speeches of recent times: Ronald Reagan's first inaugural address. Reagan had broken tradition in his inauguration in order to elevate it. For the first time he moved the ceremony around to the west side of the capital, the side of the building that looks out toward the National Mall. This permitted him to take his fellow citizens upon a tour of the National Mall as his first executive act.

Reagan spoke of several of the heroes memorialized on the Mall. Of George Washington: "a monumental man . . . of humility who came to greatness reluctantly." Of Jefferson: "The Declaration of Independence flames with his eloquence." Of Lincoln: "Whoever would understand in his heart the meaning of America will find it in the life of Abraham Lincoln."[12] From these heroes Reagan turned to the rest of us and issued a challenge. Here in America we have "unleashed the energy and individual genius of man."[13] We—meaning ordinary Americans—provide for ourselves and our family. We make the economy go. And yes, we fight the wars. Reagan quoted from the first of many private heroes that he would name in his speeches as president: Martin Treptow, who is buried in Arlington National Cemetery. He read the following from Treptow's World War I diary: "America must win this war. Therefore, I will work, I will save, I will sacrifice, I will endure, I will fight cheerfully and do my utmost, as if the issue of the whole struggle depended on me alone."[14]

---

[12] Ronald Reagan, "First Inaugural Address," (January 20, 1981), *The Inaugural Addresses of the Presidents*, ed. John Gabriel Hunt (New York: Gramercy Books, 1995), 477.

[13] Ibid., 474.

[14] Ibid., 478.

Edmund Fairfield and Ronald Reagan each asserted that in America, every citizen is a prince and a ruler. Because each is responsible, each must cultivate the virtues by which responsibilities can be discharged. These include, of course, the commercial virtues, such as industry, frugality, and honesty. They include the family virtues, such as faithfulness, devotion, and love. They include also the public virtues: justice, courage, and moderation.

The setting of Fairfield's speech was also elevated, if more rustic and not so high as Reagan's. The College was built upon the highest hill in southern Michigan. Down below was a small town. Early photographs exhibit a panorama of houses and barns and sheds, fences and livestock, muddy roads and dust in the air. The citizens gathered to hear Fairfield were local eminences, but no one of national influence was present for the dedication. They were a long way from anywhere. Yet Fairfield asserted that these people were kings, and that this college would train the kings of the future. In these surroundings, one might be tempted to think that Fairfield's high themes appeared pretentious.

But consider: In 1854, a year after Fairfield delivered his speech on "The College and the Republic," a convention of the new Republican Party was held in Jackson, Michigan, 35 miles up the road from Hillsdale. It would be the first national convention of the party that would become the majority party in the United States for more than 70 years. Fairfield and Hillsdale faculty member Austin Blair (who would later become governor of Michigan) were among the chief organizers of the convention. And the convention proved to be significant. In its proceedings are to be found the central ideas that would bring the Republican Party to power: that slavery is wrong and was condemned by the American Founders uniformly, including those Founders who were holders of slaves themselves; that the federal government has no power to eradicate slavery in states where it exists; but that it does have the power effectively to forbid the spread of slavery into the federal territories. The principles and policies articulated at the Jackson convention reflected an understanding of the Constitution as a document committed to human liberty, but also an awareness that the Constitution requires restraint.

Hillsdale's part in the momentous events of the mid-nineteenth century did not end with helping to build one of the most important political movements in American history. When civil war broke out in 1861, the Latin and Greek scholars of the Hillsdale student body showed an unsurpassed propensity to volunteer for military service. Before the war ended, over 500 young men enlisted. Sixty of them would be killed. Three would win the Congressional Medal of Honor. Three would rise to the rank of general. At least half would become officers.[15] On April 19, 1861, the Hillsdale faculty passed a resolution in favor of enforcing the laws, supporting the Constitution, and suppressing the rebellion.[16] In so doing they swept aside fears that the College would be bankrupted by the absence of its male students.

The anti-slavery credentials of the College were well-established in its earliest days. In 1847, it received a note of greeting from former president John Quincy Adams, then an anti-slavery leader in the House of Representatives. This reputation continued through the war years. In 1863, the great Frederick Douglass gave a speech on campus titled "Truth and Error," during a visit organized by the Ladies Literary Society. Edward Everett, who spoke before Lincoln at Gettysburg, was a benefactor of the Hillsdale College Library and spoke at Hillsdale in May 1862. Clinton Fisk, a Hillsdale College student, was a noteworthy supporter of the underground railroad who became a friend of Abraham Lincoln and a general in the Civil War. After the war he opened the Fisk School for Freedmen, soon to become Fisk University, in Nashville, which is today one of the most distinguished black colleges in the land. Just as the students at Hillsdale, so the students at Fisk received a classical education in those first days. They too were being prepared for self-government.

The spirit that produced the service—military, academic, and political—of Civil War-era Hillsdale students is manifest in an 1861 article by Loretta E. Crane, a Hillsdale student herself, in a publication of the Hillsdale College Ladies Literary Society, the *Souvenir*. It reads like a letter from a Spartan mother:

---

[15] Arlan K. Gilbert, *Hillsdale Honor: The Civil War Experience.* (Hillsdale, MI: Hillsdale College Press, 1994), xvi.

[16] "Hillsdale College Civil War Faculty Resolution," Hillsdale College *Standard*, April 23, 1861.

This republic, that has been the wonder and admiration of the world, must not be allowed to crumble in pieces, and become a matter of history. Every lover of liberty should go forth in the strength of right to battle for freedom and his country. In this crisis, the country calls for the assistance of every true freeman, and this call has met with a noble response. There is no shrinking from duty.

It is true, a battlefield, with the roaring of cannon, the clashing of arms, the groans of the dying and the pale faces of the dead presents no pleasing picture to the mind. But who would not rather meet this, than fill a coward's grave? That the Union may be preserved, the Constitution respected, and the flag of our country honored, is the governing principle of every true son of liberty.[17]

Today it may seem paradoxical that the federal government—the Union—should have received so large and marvelous an outpouring of support from a college to which it had given precisely nothing. It would not have seemed so to Edmund Fairfield or to Ransom Dunn, who himself lost a son in the Civil War. To them, patriotism in a just cause would have seemed the natural harvest of liberal education in a regime of limited government, a regime of local control of local matters, including education.

As Hillsdale College was building its foundation and surviving through the Civil War, changes in thought about education were beginning to emerge and gather strength elsewhere. In the twentieth century these changes would become established as the dominant practice, and both education and the workings of the Constitution would be fundamentally altered. Just as our nation developed its original constitutional forms under the influence of certain ideas, so its new and different forms have developed under new and different ideas. It is easy to see the changes in forms. To see the ideas behind them takes more digging.

---

[17] Loretta E. Crane, "War," Hillsdale College *Souvenir*, June 1861.

For most of our history the central government was powerful, but limited to a few objects. Today it is powerful, and limited almost not at all. It is hard to think of anything it may not and does not do. There are federal sidewalks in my hometown of Pocahontas, Arkansas, which lead the rare pedestrian up to rarely used but nicely appointed federal tennis courts. There are federal crops growing in Luther, Michigan.

Drive—or better, ride a motorcycle—across the heart of America on the back roads. You will come across one after another of the small towns that are scattered across the vastness. As you enter you will often see a building out of character with the rest. It is newer and built to more sumptuous standards. It exudes not grace but imposition. It is not quite a fort; it is an establishment. It is the federal building, the place from which the authority of Washington, D.C. radiates locally. The newness of the building often gives a clue that the thing it houses is new, or recently prospering. Sometimes this new activity takes over old buildings, and from that one can measure the scale of it. In little Pocahontas, which has hardly grown in population from its 6,000 citizens 40 years ago, it took over the old bank building first. Then it moved to a much bigger place, the old hospital. There one will find the Black River Area Development Corporation, whatever that is.

This change is significant. An earlier and perceptive traveler across America, Alexis de Tocqueville, noticed the importance to us of local government. He said that great nations are always able to build central assemblies, because they are big enough to produce talented people to fill them. The danger in such nations is that these assemblies will hold in contempt all attempts at local independence. Municipal assemblies, he explains, can survive only if "the institutions of a township . . . have been mixed with national ideas and habits."[18] These local assemblies of citizens constitute:

> The institutions of a township are to freedom what primary schools are to science; they put it within reach of the people; they make them taste its peaceful employ and habituate them to making use of it.[19]

---

[18] Alexis de Tocqueville, *Democracy in America*, vol. I, trans. and ed. Harvey C. Mansfield and Delba Winthrop (Chicago: University of Chicago Press, 2000), 57.
[19] Ibid.

Self-government was in Tocqueville's view connected to a disposition of mind and heart that was typically American. It had to do with the
attitude of ordinary people toward government—and not only government. Americans have an individual spirit of *independence*, meaning the
habit of being responsible for themselves and of exercising the concomitant authority. Tocqueville finds the source of this in local towns. This
spirit goes so far as to influence how we stand before or address a public
official, and the mood that comes to us when we see one:

> Often the European sees in the public official only force; the
> American sees in him right. One can therefore say that in America
> man never obeys man, but justice or law.[20]

This spirit, moreover, is productive of energy and accomplishment
in the private and the public sector alike, driven by the initiative of private citizens:

> Thus he has conceived an often exaggerated but almost always
> salutary opinion of himself. He trusts fearlessly in his own
> forces, which appear to him to suffice for everything. A particular
> person conceives the thought of some undertaking; should this
> undertaking have a direct relation to the well-being of society,
> the idea of addressing himself to the public authority to obtain
> its concurrences does not occur to him. He makes known his
> plan, offers to execute it, calls individual forces to the assistance
> of his, and struggles hand to hand against all obstacles. Often,
> doubtless, he succeeds less well than if the state were in his
> place; but in the long term the general result of all the individual
> undertakings far exceeds what the government could do.[21]

This observation by Tocqueville shows how powerfully the principles
and constitutional arrangements of a nation affect the character of the citizens. In the ancient world, the term "constitution" meant something more

---

[20] Ibid., 90.
[21] Ibid.

than a written document prescribing the arrangements of government. It meant the way of life of a people. Under a system of limited government, in which the constitutional powers do not dictate every mode of life, that, too, has the effect of shaping character and refining outlook. The restraint upon government, properly arranged and directed, breeds both restraint and assertiveness in the right degree and direction among the people.

One must ask how such a powerful and deeply embedded way of governing as Tocqueville observed here in the 1830s should have been eroded. The answer is that it took a very long time. The force that accomplished this erosion proceeded, like the original constitutional arrangements, from ideas. In education, those ideas were advanced early in the nineteenth century by educators such as Charles Brooks and Henry Barnard, and by statesmen such as James Garfield, our twentieth president and author of the legislation that founded the Department of Education. Brooks, a Massachusetts Unitarian pastor, explained the hopes of the new movement in education in a breathtaking statement:

> All children by nature have equal rights to education. A republic, by the very principles of republicanism, is socially, politically, and morally bound to see that all the talent born within its territory is developed in its natural order, the proper time, and due proportion; thus enabling every mind to make the most of itself. The republican state stands *in loco parentis* to every child, and is therefore bound to use all the means and capabilities sent by heaven for its highest aggrandizement.[22]

*****

As we have seen, the founders of America regard education as a matter of the first importance. On the other hand, they do not proclaim a "right" to it. Each of us may speak or pray with others as he pleases, and our fellow citizens may all do the same thing at the same time. These are rights readily available and natural to the human person. But many things that

---

[22] Charles Brooks, quoted in Donald R. Warren, *To Enforce Education: A History of the Founding Years of the United States Office of Education* (Detroit: Wayne State University Press, 1974), 37. Brooks wrote this in 1864.

are necessary to the human being do not fit into the same category. They may be important or even vital, and it may be important to the society that everyone enjoys them. But these factors do not by themselves establish that the thing is a right.

Compare the right to property with the idea of a right to food. Each of us is entitled to his earnings, the product of his labor. These earnings may rightly be taken by the government only with our consent and for a common and public purpose. Because we are necessitous creatures, the business of making a living is primary for us. That is one reason Madison wrote:

> The diversity in the faculties of men from which the rights of property originate, is not less an insuperable obstacle to a uniformity of interests. The protection of these faculties is the first object of government. From the protection of different and unequal faculties of acquiring property, the possession of different degrees and kinds of property immediately results; and from the influence of these on the sentiments and views of the respective proprietors ensues a division of the society into different interests and parties.[23]

Our own faculties are a natural property to us. We must use them to provide for ourselves and our loved ones. Government exists to protect these faculties and the property we acquire with them. This does not mean, however, that we have a right to food. To assert that such rights exist is to assert that another is required by his own efforts to provide them. But of course that sets up a conflict, even a war, between one citizen and another. It pits the right of each of us to the product of our own labor against the needs of our fellow citizens. To require another to labor for us that we may do well is, in fact, a form of slavery. As Abraham Lincoln said in his Second Inaugural Address: "It is strange that some men should pray to a just God to wring their bread from the sweat of other men's faces."

Thomas Jefferson had written previously:

---

[23] James Madison, *Federalist* 10, 73.

To take from one, because it is thought that his industry and that of his father's has acquired too much, in order to spare to others, who, or whose fathers have not exercised equal industry or skill, is to violate arbitrarily the first principle of association, the guarantee to everyone of a free exercise of his industry, and the fruits acquired by it.[24]

This is not to say that we can or should permit our fellow citizens to starve, especially when they are victims of misfortune. We have many duties of charity that form the basis of every civilized society. How well the weak and the unfortunate are supported is a test of any society. Our own experience has shown that a society built upon the protection of the right to property is also the most philanthropic and generous of societies. It is also the most productive of wealth, which can be deployed to help those who suffer misfortune and to raise up those who are victims of chance or of the vices of others or of themselves. But the method by which it is deployed must not be contrived so as to undercut the system of responsibility and authority fostered by the protection of property rights.

In this sense, education is like food. It is a good thing, and for happiness and good government it is a necessary thing. But it is not a natural property of the human being in the same sense as the gift of speech. Education requires effort over a long period of time. The highest forms of education require abilities not granted to every person. The "different and unequal faculties of acquiring property" are matched by the different and unequal faculties of acquiring education. The protection of those different and unequal faculties does not require that each get the same amount of education; that is no more possible to achieve than that each should have the same amount of property. The protection and encouragement of the faculty to learn requires that none be obstructed in the improvement and exercise of his mind.

Charles Brooks's idea that the republican state is the parent of every child follows from his idea that each has a right to an education. The family disappears in this conception. The rearing of children, which is the

---

[24] Thomas Jefferson, to Joseph Milligan (April 6, 1816), *The Writings of Thomas Jefferson*, vol. XIV, 466.

natural duty of parents, is a burdensome task that consumes at least a significant minority of the lives and property of the parents. The natural love they bear their children corresponds to the duty they acquire in conceiving and bearing them. The family, like the free market, is in the conception of America's Founders a vital institution. But it is also to be a private institution, able to achieve both its public and its private purposes because it is private. Woodrow Wilson, who in his political career would become the point of the spear that such men as Charles Brooks fashioned, liked to say that it was his purpose to "marry" the interest of the individual to the state. The consummation of that kind of marriage can only impair and constrict the real kind.

If the government is to stand in the place of parents in regard to the education of children, it will require new administrative methods. The chief education reformers of the nineteenth century looked to Prussia for the example of such a system. In German thought and practice they found the example for a new political system for America. Henry Barnard, who would be the first commissioner of education in the new U.S. Office of Education, founded in 1869, explained this:

> In Prussia the Minister of Education is one of the most important ministers of the State. The Department of Instruction is organized as carefully as that of War or the Treasury, and is intended to act on every district and family in the kingdom. We have not one State officer supported at the expense of the State to ascertain the condition of our schools and to give his time and mind to the improvement of these valuable institutions. No serious responsibility in respect to public education rests anywhere.

> The desultory and imperfect efforts of several hundred scattered individuals can never give a complete view of the defects of our schools or the best mode of remedying them. Hence one man familiar with the subject should traverse the whole ground, discover its actual state, compare different schools under dif-

ferent influences, ascertain the origin of the apathy and neglect so prevalent and the measures which would be at once effectual and acceptable. The energies of a single, well balanced mind should be employed in collecting and combining materials which shall give greater force and efficiency to the system.[25]

Notice the sharp contrast here with the attitude of Americans as Tocqueville observed them. To the Founders, and in American political practice until well into the twentieth century, centralization is seen as a danger. It obstructs our own efforts to care for our own interest. It denies us practice and experience in government. It thwarts our private efforts to raise our families, to run our businesses, to perform the labor by which we make our living. By this older way of thinking, centralization of these detailed matters into the power of a "single, well balanced mind" is dangerous above all because that mind is a human mind, and men are not angels. One human mind—even several human minds—cannot manage intricate localized affairs effectively. Nor, even if they could, can they be trusted with the power to do so.

The newer view of Henry Barnard, however, is a powerful force running through the middle history of our nation. Behind it looms the notion that the infinite improvement of the human being—his evolution to a higher state of perfection—is the first object both of government and of human life. Under this conception we are no longer equal souls, entitled to our rights by nature, rightly governed only by our consent. Rather we become the object of an experiment. No longer is the government to be organized to represent us. Now it will work upon us to make us better.

As these ideas were working their way into the political system, many people were of divided mind. One such person was Andrew Dickson White, founding president of Cornell University and one of the foremost academics of the late nineteenth century. He was a man who wished to preserve the old constitutional arrangements with modifications, but on principles that have more in common with the new understanding than the old. He gave a significant statement of his views on one of the

---

[25] Henry Barnard, quoted in Warren, 34. (Barnard's quotation is from an undated manuscript.)

highest ceremonial occasions in American history. This statement provides a fine example of the dilemma posed by the new ideas to the original constitutional framework.

White was a speaker at the 100th anniversary of the Constitution of the United States, September 17, 1887. Already the Constitution was the longest-surviving written constitution in human history. Already the nation living under its dominion had expanded across the plains and the mountains to the Pacific Ocean. Already it was becoming a power in the world. There had to be a grand celebration. The chief one was held in Philadelphia, the city where the nation and its Constitution were born.

The commemoration lasted three days. There were parties, rallies, and parades. There were seminars, speeches, and discussions. At the end there was a gala dinner featuring no fewer than thirteen toasts and responses, some of them lengthy. The opening remarks were given by President Grover Cleveland. Former president Rutherford B. Hayes gave the concluding remarks. Charles Francis Adams, son and grandson of Presidents John and John Quincy Adams, and Philip Sheridan, the swift and deadly Union cavalry commander, were among the speakers. From the founding of the Republic to its salvation through civil war, the great were gathered to recall and honor what had been done. In this august company, a speech was included on the subject of education by Andrew Dickson White. Nothing can better portray the importance of education to leading Americans at the midpoint of our history than the inclusion of this speech on this evening.

The theme of the night was both continuity and growth under the Constitution. White had little to say about the former. His speech began with the arresting point that nothing could seem at first sight more "remote from the Constitution of the United States than the present growth of American education." He celebrated the Constitution by moving away from it: Schools, White said, now number "hundreds of thousands," teaching "millions on millions," with "hundreds of millions of money lavished upon it by the nation, the municipalities, the rural hamlets, and with a growth of private munificence such as the world has never before seen;— and yet not a word in the Constitution provides for this growth or even foreshadows it." White conceded that "it would not be hard to prove" that "a vast educational development must follow normally and logically" from the Constitution, and that it must take "substantially its present form and no other."[26] But he did not trouble himself to provide this proof.

This "vast educational development" is, White continued, essential to the preservation of the Constitution. The American people have developed "an instinct and conviction" that they have no security for the Constitution without this "vast complex" of educational institutions. Without these institutions the people would be a mob. And "what Constitution shall curb the despotism of a mob?"[27] (One is led to wonder at this point how the Constitution can have survived the mob while this "vast complex" was building.) At last, White said, there would be atop the vast educational complex, an institution at the summit: the Bureau of Education. Here would be the "single, well-balanced mind" for which Henry Barnard had hoped (and which he would now personally direct). But it would be constrained, White assured the listeners—a servant, not a lord:

> At the centre of the whole, Congress has established a Bureau of Education. This would seem a logical outcome of our system— not its lord, but its servant, keeping, as it were, the standard time of the whole, recording the best results of experiments here and there, enabling all to profit by the example of each, and each to profit by the example of all, but without a particle of power to impose a central will.[28]

Henry Barnard might have wanted to emulate the Prussian system. But White had reservations. He feared the control of one "single, well-balanced" mind:

> It was the boast of a minister of public instruction in one of the greatest European states that at whatever hour in the day he opened his watch, he knew exactly what study was at that time occupying the attention of every scholar in that empire. Under

---

[26] Andrew Dickson White, "The Constitution and American Education," Lecture at the Centennial Banquet, in Commemoration of the Adoption of the Constitution of the United States, September 17, 1887 (Ithaca, 1887), 3.

[27] Ibid., 5.

[28] Ibid., 7.

the political system of the United States no such boast can ever
be possible. No autocrat, or bureaucrat, or mandarin can ever
thus confiscate the developing thought of the nation to the
ambition of any sect, party, or individual.[29]

Here was a step back toward the Founders. White did not mention
the Constitution in this context, but he seemed to be referring to it. The
Constitution has protections in it against autocracy, bureaucracy, or "mandarinism." White may have been willing for a vast complex to grow. He
may have been willing for a federal office to be created to "keep the standard time of the whole." But he respected the Constitution enough to
hope that central direction, or at least absolute central direction, would
not be the result. This step back toward the Founders was powerful and
moving. It must have made a strong impression upon those gathered to
celebrate the centenary of the Constitution.

White gave a reason for opposing central control. Interestingly, it is
not quite the same as the reason that prevailed among those who wrote
the Constitution a century earlier. White objected to "mandarinism" and
"stagnation" because the thought of the nation must continue to "develop." The job of the new bureau was to record "the best results of experiments here and there." The model was the scientific one of trial and error.
For White, states were now laboratories conducting "experiments." The
Founders, on the other hand, never imagined that the states would be
laboratories conducting experiments in public policy. They thought that
the job of governance required, not the invention of new methods of government, but rather the confrontation of practical problems that arise in
real events. The ends are known. The means must be adapted to circum-
stance. This is not the model of the laboratory, but the model of pru-
dence as it is known in classical literature.

In the end, White's understanding of the states as laboratories for
experiments in national policy has proved a poor defense against centralization. Indeed, it carries within itself the principle that would prescribe rather than forbid centralization. After all, once an experiment is
successful, should it not be made uniform across the country? The feder-

---

[29] Ibid., 4.

al Bureau of Education is now the United States Department of Education. Every state has its own similar department. Below them are districts, also replete with administrators. They compile reports from every school and college in their territory. They keep detailed records at every level. They write detailed standards for every phase and aspect of education. They measure local performance against those standards. The idea is preserved that local schools and colleges may practice policies that seem to them best. But substantial flows of money depend upon compliance, and often this idea is merely a fiction. The thing that Henry Barnard wished for and Andrew Dickson White believed impossible came to pass in the twentieth century. We have now the Prussian system.

1957

❖ ❖ ❖

IN 1957 the Soviet Union launched Sputnik, the first human contrivance to escape the Earth's atmosphere. Its engines were powerful enough to thrust a 36-pound satellite into orbit. Unbeknownst to its designers, it would have a similar effect on the American education system. In the Soviet mastery of rocket science, our federal government discovered lessons in administration. It did not turn to meet the challenge through the defense power, which is its own under the Constitution and was the obvious response.[1] Rather it used the situation as a lever to manage education.

When Sputnik was launched, the president of Hillsdale College was J. Donald Phillips. He had come to the College in 1952 with four main purposes: civic education, the development of religious faith, the study and practice of the best that is known in human relations, and high academic standards.[2] He was interested in faith and freedom, in morality

---

[1] The Sprague Committee (U.S. President's Committee on Information Activities Abroad) held a conference on "American reactions to crisis: examples of the Sputnik and post-Sputnik attitudes" in 1959, a few months after Sputnik. Donald Michael and Raymond Bauer analyzed polling data. They found that the general public was much less alarmed than the news media and political Washington over the launching of the Sputnik. Most people held the common sense opinion that we were not likely in the end to be taught science by the Russians. Sprague committee records, 1959–1961, Box 5, A83-10. These records are found at the Eisenhower Library in Abilene, Kansas. They are reproduced on the Internet at http://www.hq.nasa.gov/office/pao/History/sputnik/oct58.html.

[2] Arlan K. Gilbert, *The Permanent Things: Hillsdale College*, 1900–1994 (Hillsdale, MI: Hillsdale College Press, 1998), 165.

and commerce, in leadership especially of the entrepreneurial type. He was recruited amidst weak finances and with a goal to repair them. As early as 1956, the College Board of Trustees voted to increase tuition and fees rather than accept funds from the federal government. In that year the College ran a deficit of $52,500, enough to cast its survival into doubt. In 1958 President Phillips reported to the Board that he had been able to balance the budget only by deferring maintenance that would eventually become critical. More than once a local businessperson, especially the pharmacist Spike Hennessey, rescued the College from failing to make payroll.

Meanwhile the College continued its policy of equal opportunity regardless of race or sex. In 1955, a dramatic example of this arose in athletics.

In the 1950s Hillsdale College was a national football power among small colleges. Its coach in those years, Muddy Waters, is now a member of the College Football Hall of Fame. The renown his teams won on the gridiron for more than two decades was inspiriting to a college that had long known hard times. At the end of the 1955 season the Hillsdale football team was invited to play in the Tangerine Bowl in Orlando, Florida. The bowl officials extended the invitation on condition that the black players on the team not attend. The College, enjoying then the longest winning streak in college football, was delighted with the invitation and the national television exposure it would bring. Remember that money was scarce, and attention such as this might mean survival. Nonetheless, Hillsdale declined the invitation without a moment's hesitation nor a dissenting voice. Coach Waters to this day, as President Phillips until the day he died, counts this decision among his proudest achievements. It was not a difficult decision to make. It proves, as if proof is needed, that the first administration of the College that would be offered and would refuse support from the federal government had no purpose of racial discrimination.

The first consideration of federal funds by the College is found in the minutes of a meeting of the Prudential Committee[3] of Hillsdale's Board of Trustees on February 12, 1959. The motion carried unanimously: "that Hillsdale College not participate in the Student Federal Loan Program at this time." This first instinct would prevail, but only after much soul-searching, a battle of 26 years, and a decision by the Supreme Court of the United States.

The "National Defense Student Loan Fund"—contrived in response to the launching of Sputnik—was a system of subsidized loans to students. The federal taxpayer would supply 90 percent and colleges 10 percent. The colleges would be responsible for collections and would be at risk for its 10 percent. The title of the law is, of course, an attempt to find justification for it under the defense power given to Congress in Article I, Section 8 of the Constitution. (Today we have the "National *Direct* Student Loan Program." We become progressively less squeamish about constitutional justification.)

On March 28, 1959, the entire Hillsdale College Board of Trustees took up the question of whether to accept money under this program. Staff prepared a list of pros and cons. The admissions office was strongly in favor because other colleges would be offering prospective students the opportunity: In other words, the competition would be doing it. The Board reached no final decision in this initial discussion. One member stated that the proposal was in "direct opposition to the free enterprise system which we are stressing." The board agreed that if it declined to participate, "some substitute plan should be involved which would show that free enterprise is doing the job." On May 30, the Board considered a recommendation that would become its policy until 1984 when the Supreme Court intervened:

> We agree that a private college ought not to receive government
> aid, but it is our opinion that this is not government aid to the

---

[3] The Prudential or Executive Committee was established in the bylaws of the College. The earliest edition of these bylaws in the College archives shows that the Committee had been functioning at least since February 16, 1853. Likely it was established in the original bylaws from 1844.

college but to the student and that we will regret it if we do not participate in the program.

The key argument in favor of this position was that the College should not deprive needy students of this opportunity.

On this basis Hillsdale College began participation in the National Defense Student Loan Fund program and would eventually participate in other federal aid to student programs. Applications for direct aid were proposed in subsequent Board meetings in the early 1960s. They were all voted down on the principle that the College must run its affairs independently and through the free enterprise system.

As the College was agonizing over the meaning of these student loan programs for its future, an intriguing idea arose in national politics. The College noticed it immediately and sought to take advantage. On April 1, 1959, President Phillips included a passage in a letter to the Board about a bill to permit individuals, "under certain conditions, to receive a 100 percent deduction for tax purposes for gifts to educational institutions." If this bill were passed, he wrote, "Hillsdale College will benefit almost immediately.... We can raise money no easier than this." But at the June 4, 1960, meeting of the Board of Trustees, Chairman Gillespie announced the sad demise of this bill: President Eisenhower had vetoed it.[4]

In the Homestead Act of 1862, the federal government alienated an enormous resource into private hands. The Hillsdale Board was intrigued with the possibility that another huge resource, a portion of the federal tax base, might be delegated back to the taxpayers on condition that they make charitable contributions of their own. This idea arose at a turning point, when the federal government was just beginning its enormous subsidies of education, and when the attendant regulations were being formulated. This alternative approach is one among many better ideas that might have been implemented then and could be implemented still today.

---

[4] HR-6779 was vetoed by Eisenhower on June 3, 1960. It would have permitted unlimited deductions for charitable contributions to individuals who could meet two criteria. First, the sum of contributions in the current year, plus federal tax payments, must exceed 90 percent of taxable income. Second, that must be true also for eight of the ten preceding years. Eisenhower vetoed the bill on the grounds that it would operate retroactively.

Hillsdale College was forced to choose between bad options. It could forgo the subsidies being offered and the regulations that would likely come with them, in which case it would suffer a disadvantage against its competitors who took the subsidies. Or it could accept what was offered and sacrifice its principles. The College made the choice decisively in 1962 when it published its first "Declaration of Independence."[5] The key paragraphs read:

The thousands of young men and women who have studied here have been taught some fundamental truths; among these is that the freedom guaranteed them as citizens of this great country is the freedom to fulfill their dreams and aspirations without interference; that our country's greatness is the result not of government benevolence but rather of individual initiative and enterprise; that responsibility is the counterpart of independence...;

We hold these views to be as valid today as they were in 1844 despite the appearance and growth of a contrary philosophy based on government paternalism;

It is our conviction that this contrary philosophy is negatory to the traditional beliefs and teachings of Hillsdale College and is to be deplored as harmful to the continued development of our country both morally and economically.

The Board then resolved "that it be the decision of the board of trustees of Hillsdale College to reaffirm its historic independence and to resist subsidization of its affairs by the federal government in whatever form offered."

Risk was well-known to this board. They had faced financial peril many times. They knew that by this resolution they were risking the failure of the College itself. Despite that, as in the first days, and as now, they had both nerve and conviction.

---

[5] This handsome document was reaffirmed in June 1966. We reproduce the full text of the original document and its subsequent reaffirmations in Appendix V. It was reaffirmed again in October 2003, in the form of a new resolution, reproduced in Appendix VII.

The minutes of this meeting reveal that one of the trustees argued that this resolution should include the aid to students through the National Defense Student Loan Program. The College continued, however, in its conviction that this aid to students was not support for the College. It would soon prove by two dramatic actions how seriously it took the distinction between aid to students and aid to the College.

At the June 3, 1966, meeting of the Board of Trustees, a three-member committee made an extensive report on a study it had conducted. The committee had been asked to examine how the College could continue as an "outstanding liberal arts college preparing young men and women for the important task of leadership...." In particular they were asked to study trends in income and expenses. The report told a story of both good news and bad. Over the past decade the College had increased its annual income by a factor of three. Expenses had risen by factor of 2.5. The College had suffered but one annual deficit in that decade. The student body had grown significantly. This was the good news.

On the other hand, the College needed $2.5 million to meet its master plan for capital and operating improvements. Higher salaries were needed. The library needed expanding. A new classroom building was needed to house the larger student body. The budget for next year showed a need for significant increases in expenditure beyond recent experience. The committee projected deficits for every year of operations through 1970, a total of five years. In light of this grim news, the committee had examined carefully where new sources of revenue could be found.

The key new source to which the committee directed the attention of the Board was federal money. There follows in the minutes an extended discussion of the pros and cons of accepting the money. What would donors think? What strings would be attached? Was the College's previous resistance to federal money made obsolete by the fact that so many colleges were now accepting the funds? Could the College meet the requirements laid down by the federal government?

These minutes are almost nine pages long. The committee made no recommendation as to whether the College should abandon its policy of refusing direct federal aid. But it asked two questions: (1) Can we as trustees ignore these [stark] figures?; and (2) What is our obligation as trustees? Two trustees moved that the Board instruct the administration to "proceed at once with the program to obtain from federal sources all grants for which Hillsdale College may qualify to supplement our own fund-raising activities." The discussion that followed brought forth a variety of opinions.

This important matter was decided with a roll call vote, a rare thing for a nonprofit board. When the votes were counted, only two members (there were three on the committee that had compiled the report), voted in the affirmative. Sixteen voted in the negative. The motion failed. The Board then immediately passed a resolution reaffirming the policy of nondiscrimination as to race and sex that had prevailed since the founding of the College.

Again, the Hillsdale College trustees placed the College's survival at risk on a question of principle that it chose to draw itself, and in the face of grave predictions for the future. During this same period of time one college after another, including dozens that had originally refused government support, reversed themselves.

Another dramatic step was taken in a meeting of the Board in September 1969. The federal government had provided on July 1 of that year that it would now permit colleges to draw from the federal taxpayer "an amount up to three percent of the total Defense Loans made during any fiscal year" to reimburse themselves for the administrative expenses of the program. After discussion, the Board formed "a consensus that the acceptance of this offer would not be in keeping with the College's philosophy as stated in our Declaration of Independence." The motion to that effect carried by voice vote. To accept this offer would be to cross the line and accept federal taxpayer support directly to the College. Instead Hillsdale would use private resources to subsidize the administration of the student loan program.

By the end of the Phillips administration, the position of the College was manifest. It would continue its original policy of accepting students without regard to color or sex. It would continue its original mission of pursuing the liberal arts. It would continue its interest in the freedoms that are the central purpose of American society. Whatever its financial struggles, it would continue these policies without support from the federal taxpayer. President Phillips made a shining record. It would be continued under his successor, George C. Roche III.

George Roche was inaugurated president of Hillsdale College on October 9, 1971. Among the first actions taken during his administration was a reaffirmation of the College's Declaration of Independence on its tenth anniversary in 1972. Also in 1972, Congress reauthorized the Higher Education Act of 1965 for the second time. The second reauthorization established for the first time grants, as opposed to loans, to students who could demonstrate financial need.

On June 23, 1972, Congress amended the Civil Rights Act of 1964. Title IX of the amendments dealt with discrimination in educational institutions. It provided that colleges accepting federal aid must gather data on the race and sex of students and staff and report this data to the Department of Health, Education, and Welfare. Knowing that the Act would be controversial and impose complicated procedures on colleges, Congress set the Act's effective date forward three years, to July 21, 1975. After that, colleges were given three additional years, until July 21, 1978, to comply.

On October 10, 1975, the Hillsdale College Board of Trustees resolved that it would refuse to comply with Title IX. The resolution states that the College has always been independent of federal control "by consistent refusal of federal aid to education, federal grants in any and all forms of subsidy by the federal government." The federal government, it says, "now seeks to impose its control…through the subterfuge that a few of the students of Hillsdale College receive federal aid through the medium of such programs as Veterans Benefits and the National Direct Student Loan Fund." The College has "traditionally far exceeded the social benefit purported to be achieved in these regulations by natural and voluntary nondiscrimination." Therefore Hillsdale College will "hold to its traditional policy of equal opportunity without discrimination by reason of race, religion, or sex, but such nondiscrimination will be voluntary, thus preserving equality with dignity and encouraging friendship based on recognition of equal worth and mutual respect."

The Board caused this resolution to be widely published. As a result, on October 14, the College's attorney reported to the administration the "venomous attitude" reflected by federal HEW and EEOC personnel at a seminar. He warned that "the College could expect direct government suits" and the instigation indirectly of civil suits against it. His memo considered the option of applying for a hardship exemption to the new federal requirements for recordkeeping on race. But he counseled against this on the grounds that it would establish that the College was in its own eyes a recipient organization of federal funds.

President Roche wrote to David Matthews, the secretary of the Department of Health, Education, and Welfare, on November 3, 1975, stating that the College is "deeply distressed to find itself suddenly reclassified as a recipient of federal funds." The letter expressed hope that the "resultant injustice is no more than a result of bureaucratic oversight."

In 1976, the College's financial aid director, Connie Bricker, reported to Vice President Tony Fowler that new regulations were coming from the Veterans Administration. The College would now have to monitor each course and the total enrollment. If 35 percent or fewer of the students in a course, or 85 percent in the total College, did not qualify for certain federal programs, including veteran benefits, then the course would not be eligible for these benefits. This extraordinary requirement of recordkeeping by course would be necessary if the College were to continue to be eligible for the GI Bill.

In response, Hillsdale provided its resolution of October 10, 1975, to HEW. Secretary Matthews replied on March 17, 1976, saying he was glad that the College "supported the purposes of the law." He would do what he could to minimize any compromise of the College's independence. But the College was covered by the law because it participated in several student aid programs. U.S. Senator Charles Percy of Illinois wrote to HEW on behalf of Hillsdale College regarding this matter, and he received a cursory response. HEW was going forward.

In August 1976, HEW's legal counsel opined that any colleges participating in these indirect programs were "'receiving federal assistance' within the meaning of Title VI, Title IX, and Section 504." The same memo then immediately admits that "the statutory term ('receiving federal assistance') is ambiguous and the legislative histories are too sparse to settle the issue conclusively...." Nonetheless, it continued, HEW, the Department of Justice, and the judiciary had consistently concluded that the answer is yes. In other words, *the legislature has not said* whether it intended for private colleges, receiving no federal funds except through its students, to be regulated. But *the regulatory agencies decided that they should be.*[6]

On April 4, 1977, HEW sent a memorandum to the presidents of colleges and universities who had not filed their compliance forms. The memorandum included a copy of HEW form 639A and required that it be filed not later than June 3, 60 days later. On July 29, Hillsdale received a form letter from HEW signed by David S. Tatel, director of the Office for Civil Rights. This letter was made personal by typing in the title president and the address of the College in a different font than the body of the letter. It too included form 639A, which was 13 pages long and required detailed analysis and recordkeeping by the College. It required that the College demand the same analysis and recordkeeping of its subcontractors. It required that the College agree to comply with all of the many regulations being passed, both those current and any in the future.

Hillsdale College did not sign or return the form. On December 9, HEW informed the College that it would be suspending all future approvals for student aid beginning 30 days from the date of the letter. Enforcement proceedings would begin forthwith. The College could expect an administrative hearing in the near future on the charge of noncompliance. In a letter dated December 20, the College's attorney[7] made reference to "the recent oral threat by an HEW official." This official threatened to demand that all federal loans and grant funds presently in the possession of Hillsdale be placed in escrow until after a hearing. This would mean, of course, that Hillsdale would be compelled to provide services to students without the tuition payments that were being made by these federal loans. The plain purpose was to place the College in a financial bind. HEW had shown its teeth.

---

[6] OGC Staff Memorandum, attached to letter from Martin H. Gerry, director, Office for Civil Rights to George C. Roche, III, August 3, 1976.

[7] Gordon Coffman of the firm Wilkinson, Cragun & Barker of Washington, D.C.

The December 20th letter also explained that there was little precedent, and much confusing language in the law and regulations, about what would happen to Hillsdale if it continued its refusal to comply. At this stage, the College faced both threats and a deep uncertainty of what the future would hold.

On July 24, 1977, the new HEW secretary, Joseph Califano, wrote to college presidents that the "adjustment period" for colleges and universities to come to "full compliance" with the equal athletic opportunity requirements of Title IX was over. It was necessary to be in full compliance immediately. The Department had removed all doubts of the necessity to comply, he said, by a memo from its general counsel. This is the same memo quoted above that said that the legislative history was ambiguous. The general counsel, a lawyer, could look to no law that said his agency had the power to regulate Hillsdale College. He based his opinion entirely on the views and actions of the agency itself. It was then acting effectively as legislative, judicial, and executive branches all at once.

In August 1978, administrative law judge Herbert L. Perlman ruled that the College could not be made to comply with Title IX on the basis of its participation in federal student aid programs. The reviewing authority of the Office of Civil Rights of HEW overturned Judge Perlman in October 1975. Hillsdale filed suit in the Sixth Circuit Court of Appeals the day after this ruling, on October 2, 1979.

As this suit was pending, Ronald Reagan was sworn in as president in January 1981. On January 15, he appointed Hillsdale College President George Roche to a presidential education task force. On July 1, 1982, he would promote President Roche to chairman of the National Council on Education Research. In December 1982, the Sixth Circuit issued a mixed ruling favorable in part, and unfavorable in part, to Hillsdale's position. Hillsdale and Grove City College (in Pennsylvania) together appealed to the Supreme Court. The case of *Grove City* v. *Bell* (Secretary of Education Terrence Bell) ended with a ruling against Hillsdale and Grove City on February 1, 1984. The decision of the Court was overwhelming.

On May 11, 1984, President Roche reported to the Hillsdale Board of Trustees that the Supreme Court had ruled against the College, and that it was likely the College would have to "go it alone." If that were necessary, the College was strong, and it would "announce that fact loudly and clearly to the widest possible audience." Roche then read the Board resolution of October 10, 1975. He asked for its reaffirmation in light of the recent decision. The Board unanimously approved it.

In the year 1984–1985, the amount of money the College was required to find to make up for federal student aid was about $400,000 ($700,000 in today's dollars). This was a formidable sum in those days, but it has increased about seven times in real terms today.

The Board of Trustees under J. Donald Phillips had referred once to its faith, as it set out on the course of refusing this new source of largess. They had no way to know how they would make it work. But for the proposition that they must make it work for a good cause, they were willing to commit their all. This same spirit prevailed during the days of fighting with the federal government. But the College gained in strength from month to month. To begin in doubt, proceed through danger, and end up in safety and victory in a cause that is right—these are the supreme satisfactions on this earth. The College knew them under J. Donald Phillips. And it knew them again under George Roche.

When the author arrived at Hillsdale College in 2000, there was waiting for him a hefty package from the Michigan Department of Education. From time to time the Department issues an accreditation to the College. This permits the education department of the College to certify its graduates to teach in Michigan public schools. This, because of reciprocity, permits them to teach in most schools in the nation, 90 percent of the schools being public. Of course Hillsdale College has trained teachers for more than 160 years, for most of that time without any accreditation whatsoever from the State or anyone else.

The package waiting for the new president said that the College was not fully in compliance with the standards for accrediting colleges to certify teachers to teach in the public schools. The document was 35 pages long—and they were not generally exciting pages to read. Two of the complaints, among very many, were vividly clear and may stand for the rest.

The first complaint concerned Hillsdale's teaching of Western civilization. It was summed up in this passage: "In accordance with the Constitution of Hillsdale College, general studies provides students with literary and scientific principles of Western culture. (It is assumed that the intent is to point out the limitation to Western culture.)"

Notice the assumption: If Hillsdale were teaching Western culture, it could only be in an effort to show its limitations. Surely today, here in modern America, no college could study Western culture out of admiration.

The chairman of the Hillsdale Education Department, Robert Hanna, dug in his heels at this point. He replied that the State of Michigan had granted Hillsdale College "both the authority and the responsibility to act on its Charter and Mission Statement. . . ." It would only be a weakness in our program if we did not so do. The Department responded: "This weakness remains. The Hillsdale program, based on the principles of Western culture, does not incorporate global perspectives by design. It is unclear how to resolve this weakness."

The report, although full of obscurity, was presented in a convenient tabular format. One may follow along the rows and columns and track what was demanded, and what was replied, and what was said back, and so on. But there was not room in those rows and columns to make some simple points about Western civilization that were once commonplaces in education. They are worth making here.

Western civilization is the product of two things coming together. The first is Biblical religion, and the second is Socratic philosophy. That is why the Hillsdale mission statement calls the College "a trustee of modern man's intellectual and spiritual heritage from the Judeo-Christian faith and Greco-Roman culture." A shorter way to say the same thing is that the West can be understood as the confluence of Jerusalem and Athens.

There are many significant differences between the calls that come forth from Jerusalem and from Athens, but they have some essential things in common. The one most relevant to Hillsdale College's correspondence with the Michigan Department of Education is how they conceive the human being. The idea of Jerusalem is that there is but one God for all human beings. The idea of Athens is that the search for the good for man must seek it for man as man, not man as Athenian, or Greek, or even Westerner.

The Jews and the Christians worship a God who is the God of all, everywhere, and who regards all, everywhere, impartially. This God is "no respecter of persons." It is true that this God has chosen a people, but in His covenant with them, He makes plain that: "[I]n thy seed shall all the nations of the earth be blessed; because thou hast obeyed my voice."[8] Similarly, Socrates asks persistently to be shown the good, true, and beautiful things as they are, absolutely and in their essence. Universality is essential to the investigation he undertakes.

This confluence of universal monotheism and universal philosophy is very valuable. It may be uniquely valuable. It may be superior to anything found in the East. Even if it is, it teaches that the potential for things of equal value and meaning must be present in the East, and also in the North and the South, so long as human beings are living in them. If those things have not developed there, the reasons are accidental, and not essential to the quality of the people who live in those places.

Another lesson follows too: One would not need necessarily to study both the East and the West, the North and the South, to find out the things that are required of us by God, nor to discover by our reason the things that are good, true, and beautiful in essence. There is not time to learn all languages. There is not time to read all books. In the greatest of books, there are lessons for a lifetime, and those lessons are not in any sense narrow or parochial. On the contrary, they are specifically global and universal. One might well read the books of the East or the North or the South with great profit. But it would be better to read a few books carefully, wherever they may have been written, than to read many books lightly.

The Department of Education's criticism of the Hillsdale education program was that it failed to make "global and multicultural perspectives permeate the curriculum." In another place we were criticized for failing to mention "multiculturalism sufficiently." But in fact, multiculturalism is thin gruel for the mind. It begins with the premise that all cultures, whatever their differences, are equally worthy. It achieves this by calling into question the criteria by which culture may be judged. At a church vestry meeting I once made the comment that some cultures are evil. Some of

---

[8] The Lord speaking to Abraham, Genesis 22:18.

my colleagues, especially the most educated ones, gasped to hear such a thing. I asked if the culture that prevailed in Germany between late 1933 and early 1945 would be called evil. Everyone relaxed. It is safe still to condemn Nazism, though the philosophical and moral ground for doing so is eroding beneath our feet.

This attempt to denigrate Western civilization in the name of multiculturalism reaches very far now. Wherever there are schools of education, programs are regulated by central departments that define curricula and oversee the closest details of the programs' functioning. A young person of eighteen going off to college will be taught things that are commanded in state capitals and in Washington. He will not know that many of the most precious achievements of the human mind are forbidden him under these commandments. Standards in our public schools are embarrassingly low. The longer our students stay in them, the further they fall behind most of the rest of the world. The ultimate explanation for this disaster can be found in the principle that all achievements of culture are equally worthy, which means necessarily that they are also equally unworthy.

The second transgression of Hillsdale College, according to the Michigan Department of Education, has to do with race, or rather with "composition of candidates" ("candidates" refers to the students enrolled in our education program). In short, our "student body is not culturally diverse and there is no plan to change that status."

Now, at Hillsdale College we do not—nor have we ever—asked any applicant for admission what his race might be. We have no records on this subject, and we have never had them. The Michigan Department of Education was not happy with this, and so they sent several observers down to the campus with clipboards to walk about and count the people they saw by color. In response to this outrage, I brought up the things that Frederick Douglass had said on this subject. Douglass has come into our story before. He was a runaway slave. After his escape, he had to live in England for several years to protect himself from the fugitive slave laws, under which he would be returned to servitude if found in the North. Having righteous indignation in plenitude, he was however a man without bitterness.

Douglass came to speak at Hillsdale as an honored and celebrated guest in the middle of the Civil War. There were many places in the North where he would not have been welcome in that day. In the South, he would have been arrested on sight. We have a list of the young men who gave their lives to vindicate the rights of Frederick Douglass, and also their own rights. The list is very long for a college this size.

As the Civil War was ending, Douglass was asked what should be done on behalf of the freed slaves. How could they be helped? He responded with a mixture of magnanimity and good principle:

> [I]n regard to the colored people, there is always more that is benevolent, I perceive, than just, manifested towards us. What I ask for the negro is not benevolence, not pity, not sympathy, but simply justice. The American people have always been anxious to know what they shall do with us.... I have had but one answer from the beginning. Do nothing with us! Your doing with us has already played the mischief with us. Do nothing with us! If the apples will not remain on the tree of their own strength, if they are worm-eaten at the core, if they are early ripe and disposed to fall, let them fall!... And if the negro cannot stand on his own legs, let him fall also. All I ask is, give him a chance to stand on his own legs! Let him alone!... [Y]our interference is doing him positive injury.[9]

This quotation is not difficult to find, in part because it is reprinted in the papers of Frederick Douglass, but also because it is reprinted as the second paragraph in the dissent of Supreme Court Justice Clarence Thomas in the recent case of *Grutter* v. *Bollinger*.[10] This case concerned the University of Michigan, which is located about 70 miles from Hillsdale, and its own practice of "counting by race" in admitting students.

Hillsdale College does not follow race-based policies like those at the University of Michigan. Our Articles of Association support "civil and

---

[9] Frederick Douglass, "What the Black Man Wants: An Address Delivered in Boston, Massachusetts, 26 January 1865, reprinted in *The Frederick Douglass Papers*, vol. 4, J. Blassingame and J. McKivigan, ed. (New Haven, CT: Yale University Press, 1991), 59, 68.

[10] 539 U.S. 306, 348 (2003) (Thomas, J., concurring in part, dissenting in part).

religious freedom and intelligent piety." The method of support is "sound learning." These are goods available and right for all human beings. It does not matter their size or their color or their sex.

"Sound learning," as we have already noted, is not equally available to everyone. At the highest level, it requires the possession of certain capacities that are not ubiquitous among human beings. The possession or lack of these capacities has however nothing to do with size or color or sex. This is why the founders of Hillsdale College—and for all I know those of the University of Michigan—promised at the beginning to admit students without regard to color or sex.

The University of Michigan stands on a different footing than Hillsdale College in one important respect. It is a function of the people of the State of Michigan, who are part of the people of the United States. The University of Michigan is an official act of those people and has the force of law behind it. Michigan and the United States were certainly both founded according to the same promise upon which our College was born. They both stray from it these days, especially in their universities. Indeed, their universities lead them to stray.

Neither from the point of view of the nature of the human being, nor from the point of view of the highest goal of education, does it make the slightest difference what color someone is. Any other view destroys the possibility of knowledge in the human being, because it reduces the human being to accidental and material characteristics. That is why the founders of our College, like the great Frederick Douglass, believed that we ought not to take account of color. That is why we do not do so even to this day. Nor, God preserving us, will we do so in the future.

These modern stories of Hillsdale College and government regulation exhibit something the Founders of our nation understood and against which they warned. Today local matters are subject to intricate and detailed central control. The waste resulting from this system is massive, but it is not the worst thing. The worst thing is the spirit and direction of that control. The passion that animates it is destructive of the highest and best things in the tradition of American education. It makes war directly upon them. That war is clear in the case of Hillsdale College for the simple reason that it fights back.

2004

❖ ❖ ❖

WE HAVE EXAMINED the past and the present. We find in the past a college born that supported the central principles of America. It supported them by studying the classic books, what Jefferson called the "elemental books of public right." Most colleges did so at the time. Hillsdale College did so with particular intensity.

We find that Hillsdale College gave signal support to its country. It asked nothing in return. It was a shining example of the public as well as the private benefits of self-government and liberal education.

We find that a century and a half later things had changed. They had changed both in government and in education. The "elemental books of public right" had fallen out of favor at most colleges. Hillsdale College still clung to them. For its part, the government had begun to offer subsidies where none had been requested, and to make demands where none were justified.

We find that Hillsdale College stood defiantly by its old ideas that it is a place where leaders are trained, and that the training of leaders should not be done by the government itself; that the government should not exceed the authority granted to it by a sovereign people; and, finally, that people ought not to be counted by the color of their skin, above all in education.

We find that because of these changes the College came into conflict with the government and with most of its sister colleges. The conflict was about the scope of the government. It was also about the nature of education and, ultimately, the nature of man. These things are connected.

What does the future hold?

During the academic year 2004–2005, shortly after this book is published, it is probable that the Higher Education Act of 1965 will be authorized for the eighth time. For the first time it will be reauthorized under the control not of the party that originated it but of The Other Party. The Other Party has some new ideas. It advances those ideas in the face of an old situation. It faces enormous demands from the "stakeholders" for more. It holds the slimmest majority in the government, symptomatic of a nation deeply and evenly divided. Those who report the news, themselves the products of the colleges and universities that hold the biggest stake, will, for the most part, say what is helpful to the demand for more.

These stakeholders are a mighty force. They include especially the elite universities, but also nearly all of their sister institutions. Their position on the reauthorization is that they should be given more money, and they should be permitted to do what they please with it. There are regulations governing them that run to thousands of pages. These should be relaxed. Or they should be allowed to write new ones more to their liking. They claim to represent the cause of education itself. They are the experts who should be permitted to run the matter. The business of the government is to get the money for them from the patient taxpayer, even if he grows impatient.

These stakeholders are a little embarrassed, but not much, by the fact that their leading employees, the faculty members, vote and work in overwhelming majority for one party (not The Other Party). Also their curricula becomes increasingly a training ground for every kind of radical, dangerous, and silly cause. Conservatives are generally not welcome among them. These facts are pronounced. They are a scandal. They do not scandalize only because custom has inured and power has cowed us.

This is the difficult situation with which The Other Party will now attempt to cope. It has new ideas, which have some virtues and also some problems. One of its proposed bills seeks to control costs, a good thing. Federal subsidies tend to drive up the cost of a college education. For one thing, tuition is a factor in calculating student eligibility for federal subsidies. If a college has a higher tuition, then the "need factor" for any given student enrolled there will be higher. It is not surprising that colleges raise tuition faster than the rate of inflation, faster even than Congress can vote additional money to them.

The cost control bill would penalize colleges that raise their tuition more than twice the rate of inflation. This is a system of price controls. Of course the colleges will be artful in evading these controls, and there will be plenty of opportunity. Tuition is a complicated matter; few students actually pay the stated rate. Colleges give scholarships, grants, loans, and other forms of discount. If this system is to be regulated, it must be regulated in great detail, much as Medicare is regulated. The bureaucracies that have already written thousands of pages or regulations will now write thousands more. There will be no end to the mess, just as there no end to the mess in Medicare.

After all is said and done, the simple truth will remain that if one wishes to bring supply and demand into accord, he must let prices do it. But prices must be set not by government, but by the interplay of supply and demand itself. Otherwise they will be very inefficient.

Another proposed bill—more intelligent and ambitious about the content of education, where the problem really lies—would impose a new theory. The bill is not drafted to be mandatory. It states the "sense of the Congress." It addresses bias in education.

Goodness knows that the tendency of college professors and administrators to adhere to the politics of modern liberalism is overwhelming. Political correctness is rampant. Just as costs are running out of control, so ideology is running out of control on college campuses. One must not, if he has any conservative leaning, let that fact be known. It is only sensible, one would think, to try to do something about this sorry situation.

The trouble is in the theory behind the proposed "Academic Bill of Rights." It is taken from the American Association of University Professors: "[T]here is no humanly accessible truth that is not in principle open to challenge, and...no party or intellectual faction has a monopoly on wisdom." And "no political, ideological, or religious orthodoxy should be imposed on professors and researcher. . . ." Furthermore,"curricula and reading lists in the humanities and social sciences will respect the uncertainty and unsettled character of all human knowledge in these areas and provide students with dissenting sources and viewpoints. . . ."

There is an important element of truth in these statements. They are themselves a theory of education, and they are not the only one. Their central idea is that we do not know, and because we do not know every opinion should be represented. Or to be more fair: Every serious, reasoned opinion by trained and qualified people should be represented.

This is the theory that no theory can be proved to be true. The contradiction is easy to see. One need only ask, what about this theory? And furthermore, what about the conclusion you draw from it? How do we know, if we do not know, that a variety of views is good? Good people today often support freedom on the premise that truth like beauty is in the eyes of the beholder. Nietzsche wrote, on the other hand, that "nothing is true, and so everything is permitted."

Is Nietzsche wrong about this? Is he wrong because of some absolute truth? If there is such an absolute truth, then why do we base our support of diversity on the ground that there is no absolute? What if I say Nietzsche is wrong because I do not like what he says? If likes and dislikes are the standard, then Nietzsche's are as good as mine. Perhaps I will take the view that Nietzsche can teach what he wants, and I will teach what I want. But what of the man who does not think that is the right thing to do? What if he reads Nietzsche and gets the idea that we ought to train the young to create and express a new truth, a truth that encompasses all the truths that have gone before and also surpasses them? They must have the "will to power." They must eradicate whatever stands in the way.

We cannot let this man organize the university. He would eradicate diversity. So we must refuse to do what he says. In so doing, we make a decision against him. We impose our will over his. To that extent, we have asserted that he is wrong. We have violated the principle of diversity.

That is one problem with the theory of the "Academic Bill of Rights." Another resides in the nature of the educational enterprise itself. That enterprise is continuous from the cradle to mature and reflective adult. The early parts are related to the later ones. The early parts begin in habit and proceed through teaching the child, or adolescent, or young adult what to like and what to dislike. This must all be done in the light of things that are better, things better in reality, and beyond question. Training in habit means training for service to the good. Even at the advanced level education requires a faith that something good and true can be found. Otherwise the work is itself vain. Vain tasks are not prosecuted with vigor.

I will give an example from my own life. It has to do with what will seem at first glance the least innovative of academic undertakings, the reading of an old book. The book is Aristotle's *Nicomachean Ethics*. The *Ethics* begins with this sentence:

> Every art and every inquiry, and likewise every action and choice, seems to aim at some good, and hence it has been beautifully said that the good is that at which all things aim.[1]

I read this sentence on the first day of the first course I had in graduate school. The professor in that course, the brilliant and bellicose Harry Jaffa, would prove to be of immense importance in my life. He took two weeks to get us through this first sentence. He would teach us that it involves high and complicated matters. The Greek nouns in the sentence, we would learn, comprehend every kind of voluntary human action. The sentence amounts to the assertion that all human purposeful activity, including thought, aims at the good. Can that be true? What of the murderer or the thief? What of the tyrant or the peculator? What of the sophist or the liar? And anyway what is this "good"? What if one is wrong about it? What does it matter if one aims for it, if he is wrong about it? These are difficult matters to resolve, and they are only the beginning of the difficulties. We spent a semester reading Book I of the *Ethics*. We did not get to the last nine books.

Just before we read this opening sentence for the first time, Professor Jaffa made a little speech to begin the class. He said that when professors get as old as he (he was then in his mid-fifties), they begin to compile a list of the one hundred greatest books. Life is too short, he said, to read one

---

[1] Aristotle, *Nicomachean Ethics*, trans. Joe Sachs (Newburyport, MA: Focus Publishing, 2002), 1.

hundred great books carefully. They require too much attention. Human understanding is too limited to master one hundred works by the greatest writers. This book, the *Ethics*, he said, is one of the *three* greatest books.

The effect of this speech upon us students went much further than to make us think that Aristotle's *Ethics* is a valuable book. We did think that. More important even than that important thing, we thought that an *old* book can be valuable, or rather we thought that a book can be of permanent or abiding value. We thought that a book can be so valuable as to justify devoting one's life to it. It can contain a jewel so precious that one should order his existence to find it, and indeed an existence so ordered is the highest kind of existence possible to the human being.

At the moment Professor Jaffa said this, there came over us, not a doubt, but a reverence. We began our inquiry not in doubt, but in belief and wonder. We did not set out to discover our own thoughts, still less our feelings. We set out to find something quite outside ourselves that could help us know the meaning of ourselves and of everything else. We did not even stop to think that if life is too short to read a hundred great books carefully, how can we know which are the best? That did not matter then and it does not matter now. What matters is that some books do exist that can repay that kind of devotion and scrutiny.

Of course doubt was there, too, and inescapable. It was sewn as deeply into the nature of the situation as was reverence. First of all the *Ethics* is an old book. It was written before the birth of Jesus. It was written by a Greek, not an American. At the time of its writing, there was no America, no polity devoted to the equality of rights. There was no separation of church and state. Technology was known, but Aristotle taught that it must be controlled and managed—all the powerful arts must be—to support the good of the state. But "state" does not cover the real meaning of the term "polis," which is a much more comprehensive thing. We spent weeks looking for a meaning of this term "polis."

We could not begin to read *Ethics* except by stepping outside ourselves and our time. We were being led through the book by a man who believes that the United States, with its system of limited government founded upon consent, is the best possible form of government "in the context of Western Civilization." Here is another statement that one could spend a lifetime understanding. Because of his understanding of this statement, Professor Jaffa's loyalty to the American Revolution, and to its defender Lincoln, is a flame. His investigations of it have proceeded for years. How does this compare and relate to his love of this old book, the *Ethics* of Aristotle, which seems so completely different? What is one to make of all this?

Reverence and wonder, doubt and controversy seem to go together right from the start. Because this doubt and controversy is so deep, we need reverence merely to make a good beginning, much less to sustain the effort. To search for the high things leads one on a hard climb. One cannot begin, much less sustain, the climb unless he thinks he is going *up*. He must think that there is an *up*. If there is up, there must be down. If there is higher, there must be lower. The search for truth and beauty and good involves the ranking of things. It emphatically does not involve putting all things on the same rank.

Because climbing is difficult, it is bound to be attended with error, frequent and often egregious. Opinions abound amidst the confusion. Understanding comes slowly and painfully. During our class on the *Ethics*, we students studied into the night, talked over long dinners, sharpened and honed our thoughts and—much more—our questions. Come to Hillsdale College and you will see the same thing.

Great learning begins not in doubt alone, but in belief and wonder. To be guided by wonder is to believe that wonder can be satisfied. It is not sufficient to believe that there are intellectual factions, and that they all have the same claim and always will. We do not need Congress to teach us about doubt and difference. Nor do we need it to tell us we cannot find the truth.

Enough of my own experience and my own teacher. Look at examples from another great teacher. C. S. Lewis is a titan of the twentieth century. Lewis was British; Harry Jaffa is American. Lewis taught literature; Jaffa politics.[2]

---

[2] Professor Jaffa will be cross if I do not mention that he studied literature as an undergraduate at Yale. He writes about Shakespeare with love and understanding. Of *Pride and Prejudice* he cannot stop talking.

Lewis studied mostly the medieval and renaissance worlds; Jaffa mostly the classical and American. Lewis is a great Christian apologist; Jaffa, a Jew.

Here are two different sorts, but they have some similar things to say. One of Lewis's finest works begins with a story about a school book, which he calls The Green Book.[3] The book tells the story of two men at a waterfall. One man says that the waterfall is pretty, and the other says it is sublime. Coleridge, the poet, overhears the statements and regards the first with disgust. The authors of The Green Book differ from Coleridge. They say that the first man at the waterfall "appears to be saying something very important about something; and actually [he is] only saying something about [his] own feelings." The waterfall, according to these textbook authors, has no properties that a man can objectively describe. One man's opinion about the waterfall is just as good as the next man's, because no man can have a true opinion. Here is the "Academic Bill of Rights" in capsule.

Lewis writes that the textbook has cut the student off from the moving power and the high purpose of literature, namely its ability to reflect in the human soul the high and fine things outside it. It also, says Lewis, destroys any effort to teach the virtues to the young or to sustain them in ourselves:

> The operation of The Green Book and its kind is to produce what may be called Men without Chests. It is an outrage that they should be commonly spoken of as Intellectuals. This gives them the chance to say that he who attacks them attacks Intelligence. It is not so. They are not distinguished from other men by any unusual skill in finding truth nor any virginal ardour to pursue her. Indeed it would be strange if they were: a persevering devotion to truth, a nice sense of intellectual honour, cannot be long maintained without the aid of a sentiment which [the authors] could debunk as easily as any other. It is not excess of thought but defect of fertile and generous emotion that marks them out. Their heads are no bigger than the ordinary: it is the atrophy of the chest beneath them that makes them seem so.[4]

---

[3] The Abolition of Man, first published in 1944. I read this book first under the instruction of another teacher to whom I have a great debt, Harry Neumann.

[4] C. S. Lewis, The Abolition of Man (San Francisco: Harper, 2001), 25.

In other words it is important to education that students learn to love the things that are good and high. To do that, they must believe that there are such things. It is no disservice to the objectivity of students to teach them this. They will be required to give an account of these things, and it will not be easy to do. They will have to think, and think hard. They will not think hard unless they think they have something good to think about.

Lewis concludes this book with several pages of moral precepts from various cultures. Throughout the book he calls such things the *Tao*, meaning what we call in English Nature or Right. He uses the Chinese term, and the examples from many cultures, in order to build up the idea that the moral things can be known and that they transcend locality and culture.

This is a theme and a device that recurs in the works of this great teacher and scholar. His radio addresses broadcast during the Second World War in Britain, now published as *Mere Christianity*, began with a story about people on a bus. He showed that the arguments between and among them indicate an underlying agreement about morality. "You took my seat," is not followed by, "Yes, what of it?" Instead the reply is "No, I was here first." They argue, but they agree upon the standard by which the matter should be judged. Moral knowledge, he wishes us to know, is solid and hard to deny.

In his novel *That Hideous Strength*, Lewis describes Mark Studdock, a scholar who represents among other things academic relativism. Studdock rethinks his position when he falls into the hands of people who wish to destroy entirely his sense of right and wrong, his sensibility, in order to make him a servant of evil. They force him to look at things that are crooked, out of proportion, and askew. But these crooked things only raise in his mind "the straight and the normal."[5]

Students who do not believe there is such a thing as "the straight and the normal" will not be moved to search for it.

There are examples too in the history of our own nation, in the predecessors of those public officers who now propose the "Academic Bill of

---

[5] C. S. Lewis, *That Hideous Strength* (New York: Scribner, 1996), 307.

Rights." The United States began in 1776 with the assertion that there is such a thing as a "self-evident truth." This has been as controversial at various points in the past as it is today. It was controversial with King George III and his ministers. The "Academic Bill of Rights" speaks of "organizational neutrality" for colleges among all the points of view. Should a college devoted to the principles of "civil and religious freedom and intelligent piety" be neutral among those who would protect and those who would destroy these good things?

In the twentieth century Marx and his siblings and progeny in politics and the academic world gave rise to many movements that denied the natural rights of every human being. There was the Gulag in the Soviet Union. There were the death camps in Germany and Poland. Some distinguished academics in the Soviet Union and in Germany—and in many other places—supported them. Some do still. Is it necessary for a college to employ people who teach these doctrines? Will the Congress condemn the college that refuses?

James Madison was a revolutionary. More than any man, he was the author of the Constitution, the same Constitution that the members of Congress have sworn on their personal honor to uphold. His closest political colleague was Thomas Jefferson, another revolutionary, and the chief author of the Declaration of Independence. These were people who put their lives on the line in a violent rebellion against authority. They wished that same spirit of liberty to live in those who would follow them. Jefferson and Madison engaged in a correspondence between them about the curriculum of the University of Virginia School of Law, a training ground for future leaders. Madison wrote in this regard: "It is certainly very material that the true doctrines of liberty, as exemplified in our Political System, should be inculcated on those who are to sustain and may administer it."[6]

Notice the use of the term "inculcated." It comes from a Latin term meaning to tread or press in. Madison does not mean in writing this that students should be trampled. He means instead that education, if it is to liberate, must be elevated and thorough.

---

[6] James Madison, to Thomas Jefferson (February 8, 1825), The Republic of Letters: The Correspondence between Thomas Jefferson and James Madison, 1776–1826, vol. 3, ed. James Morton Smith (New York: W. W. Norton, 1995), 1924.

The Other Party's "Academic Bill of Rights" says that no political or religious orthodoxy should prevail in a university, and in the sense in which they mean it, perhaps it is so. But Madison writes in this same letter:

> After all, the most effectual safeguard against radical intrusions into the School of Politics, will be an Able and Orthodox Professor, whose course of instruction will be an example to his successors, and may carry with it a sanction from the Visitors.[7]

To Madison, liberty is an achievement for which man has struggled through his long history. It has been achieved in America because Providence has smiled upon our efforts. He has given us a land that is fruitful and naturally strong. God has given us a people who learned discipline and charity through caring for themselves and others. He has given us the principles of freedom, which require the closest study, because they involve the soul of man and its place in nature. These are the great themes of the life of James Madison. For them he risked his life. For them he studied and worked to exhaustion, year after year. For them he argued in Philadelphia when all was at stake and, through the writing of the Constitution, all came right.

Madison and Jefferson wanted future generations of Americans to study those same principles of human freedom under the instruction of people who believe in them. If they are studied seriously, the objections to them will be revealed and all the arguments exposed. At the same time their study will not be serious unless it includes their admiration.

Education seems both to begin and to proceed, then, in the admiration of nobility, beauty, and truth, even as it is the search for them. The chance to err must be protected, but not on the ground that it is cannot be distinguished from truth. A federal law, prescribing a set of principles for every college in the land, is no true guardian even of the diversity it proclaims. It would rather destroy what is best and highest in liberal education by denying the ground on which it stands. There is not much of it left. It does not need Congress hammering it with another blow.

---

[7] Ibid., 1925.

It is not necessary to believe that every college should be organized in the way that Jefferson and Madison proposed. There are many thousdands of colleges and universities in the United States. There is no reason why the federal government should tell them all to abide by the same theory, be it modern academic relativism or the doctrines of the natural law that the Founders supported (but did not prescribe to every college). The uniformity that reigns in the university today cannot be fixed by the Congress of the United States. Certainly not as that body operates today.

How then can it be fixed? Consider three situations, two of one kind and one of another. The choice before us is exhibited in the difference between them.

In the first scene a man of eloquence and stubborn conviction sets out on a horse to ride into the winter. Already he has moved his family to the frontier. He lives in a world where people scratch out a living on land they treasure as their own. It is precisely to treasure their own land that they came to the frontier. This man is like those farmers and not like them. He chooses not to plow but to learn, to pray, to teach, and to preach. In that place at that time, it is a calling that requires iron in the soul. It requires that he benefit people who live under hardship. Since these people have almost nothing to spare, it requires that the benefit he does them be almost as real and precious to them as food for their children. He has chosen to depend upon them, and to repay their dependence upon him.

This man has made a commitment to the people in the town where his college has moved. It requires him to ask these farmers, scratching their subsistence from the soil, for a part of that subsistence. He takes years of a life that will prove to be long, but was likely to be short, to fulfill his commitment. He makes a pact with those farmers that forms for him yet another commitment, one that he will spend the rest of his life keeping. The College has a mission. He tells them it will serve that mission true.

That is the first scene.

The second scene is in a board room. One of those present has given more than he can spare, and more than once, so that the College he helps to govern can continue to operate. A much richer man from the big city nearby has headed a committee. The committee has done a study. It says that the College is on a downward spiral. There is reason for fear and gloom. The committee has cast about for another way to make do. It can find but one, a bright and shining hope. Education is important, and the taxpayer is willing to help. Yes, the government will ask certain things in return. But the College believes in some of them and others can be abided. So let us reverse ourselves and take the money. We must do it for the College. If it fails we are responsible.

Sixteen members of the board hear this speech and then vote no. Only two vote yes. The sixteen all know what it will cost them. They know that they are risking the College, and that is a heavier burden to carry than any involving their own resources. A few years before, at a similar meeting, they have put in the minutes a prayer that the College will survive. They repeat that prayer now.

That is the second scene.

In the third scene a person of good will, overworked and often weary, reads the minutes of a departmental meeting that was held in a little college to the south. He has many such colleges and departments under his charge, and many such minutes to read. He is a talented person who came to the work for the love of learning and the wish to serve. He has never been to the college whose minutes he reads, or maybe only once. He has not time to go to regularly to the colleges under his charge. He will likely never meet the students at any of them.

He notices that in one set of minutes something has been done, but in later minutes the results of that thing, whatever it is, have not been written down. This is a breach. He notes it.

He notes also that the College does not keep records of the color of its students and staff. He does not know the story of the College very well, only that it is "conservative" and different. He has not read the rolls of those who died for the principle that Frederick Douglass, the most greatly honored guest at the College in a century and a half, announced on that very campus. His office sends some people down to the college with clipboards to count the colors they see. He does not know that this is the specific evil that the founders of the College gave their sons to eradicate. He is unaware of the insult this pays to people of every color who are counted.

He notices that the College teaches Western civilization. This is a breach. He notes it.

That is the third scene.

Think of the first two scenes as a form of government in which responsibility and authority are related as one to one. The people involved give their lives to the success of the enterprise. Of course they are not saints; they have their failings aplenty. Also they are short of money. Many times people like them actually fail at what they do. Those are the chances of life.

Because the College is short of money, the students must do without. Those who work at the College long to have more to give the students and more for themselves. They work to get it. Meanwhile they make do with what they have.

At any given moment their efforts seem small and insignificant. But at key moments in history, particular ones of them are in particular places that matter. Some of them are on a battlefield in Pennsylvania when the Union is at stake. Some of them walk the halls of Congress, in the minority often, but doing what is right from year to year and in ways that make a difference. Great numbers of them start businesses, teach school, practice law and medicine, work in laboratories, help to run their communities, raise their families, care for those around them.

This is a form of government. It is what was called self-government for most of our history. It does not feature any detailed orders from above. Laws are few, simple, and general. Local people decide for themselves the things of greatest relevance to themselves. The first two scenes exemplify that form of government at its best.

The first two scenes are also a way of education. The combination of its abstractness and the concrete necessities surrounding it may appear ridiculous. Who are you to be studying a 3,000-year-old book when you do not have enough money to heat your room (or, today, to build a proper student union)? How can you support these great civic causes you proclaim when you read things written before those causes had been born?

It is not, however, ridiculous. The students and faculty have plenty of complaints, and they make them. But at the same time they value above all else in the world what they do. They pay a price for it because it is precious, and they know it is precious because they pay a price. They do not study high things because it is high fashion to do so. They do it not with the extra but with the first resources they have. They have just enough leisure to do it, and not a whit more. They value it. They do it intensely.

The third scene is not a way of education but a way of government. It locates power in the hands of people who are mostly, and, for the time being, blessedly well-meaning. But they have little contact with the things they govern and none with the people who provide the resources. The people who provide the resources—the taxpayers—do not even know they are providing the resources.

The first two scenes are full of trouble and challenge. They are the specific things that our Fathers in the Revolution fought to achieve for us. They are the expression of the American constitutional system. They are examples of self-government, particularly noble examples, but of a kind that are compounded infinitely through the history and, to a lesser extent, the contemporary practice of our nation.

The third scene is not the expression of, but the danger to America's constitutional system. Nor is it an expression of liberal education; it does not know what that means. Andrew Dickson White, having lost contact with the full meaning of our constitutional system, still had part of the meaning. He called this new thing, this new centralized bureaucracy, "mandarinism."

Last Christmas at the Field Museum in Chicago, a wonderful place especially to take children, there was an exhibit of the possessions and life of Qianlong, the greatest of the Chinese Emperors. The exhibit told a glorious tale. Qianlong was very rich, and he wielded great power after his father conquered China.

The exhibit was at some pains to say what a just ruler the man was. He loved his people. He was energetic and caring in their service. In one place the exhibit materials made the point that the glories of a great national China, as exemplified by the benevolent Qianlong, have been restored to China today. Of course the people who rule that great national China today had to give permission for the exhibit to visit Chicago. Likely they had some influence over what the exhibit said. That would explain some things about it.

A mural in the exhibit shows the Great Emperor visiting a town. The entire population of the town is ranged before him. He is being carried in an ornate chair by hefty men. All the townspeople are on their knees.

That is the meaning of mandarinism. One need only look in the *Encyclopedia Britannica* to see that not quite everything was rosy and fine during the rule of Qianlong in China. Nor is everything fine there today. China was, and still is, ruled by mandarinism. That is one reason why the exhibit was not candid about the evils that came under the regime of Qianlong.

The Founders of our nation did not intend to establish mandarinism. That is why they taught that responsibility and authority ought to go together. That is why they did not give the federal government power to manage education. It was too important for that. For the sake of education, and for the sake of freedom, the federal government should get out of it.

Powers and interests are so arranged today that it seems hopeless that any good can be done. The modern research university has replaced the liberal arts college as the standard bearer in education. It is entrenched, immovable, almost almighty. Its force is enrolled nearly exclusively on one side of the political spectrum. Politicians bask in its favor or quail before its frown. Bureaucrats work with it hand in hand.

Perhaps the time has past when politicians of either party should seek to regulate this behemoth. The answer may be less rather than more involvement. It may be time, or long past time, for us to demonstrate what we are by another great act of delegation, another great episode in which the most powerful make treasures available to individuals in their multitude, to husband and direct as seems best to them. In the Northwest Ordinance, the precious resource of Western lands was sold outright to ordinary folk, without condition. The boldest and most persistent people in the world had crossed the ocean and braved a wilderness to secure land. The government owned the land. It gave it up.

In the Homestead Act, the government did the same thing, but this time it did not charge a fee. Once again a wonderful asset was given away. It was not given to barons and earls. It was not given to friends of those in power. There was no chance for bureaucrats to say who got what. There was one grand act of disposition, the same for one and all.

In 1959 the germ of an idea passed Congress, but it was vetoed in the White House. The idea was that ordinary folk could give their money to colleges instead of to the government. The great asset that government holds today, greater even than its vast holdings of land, is the enormous claim it holds upon the wealth and income of the American people. There is no good reason why the people cannot give that money away themselves. Some way should be found.

Of course the powers of modern education will object to this. They will say that this is easy for Hillsdale College to recommend. We have found a way to survive without money from the taxpayer. The answer to that is— yes, with great difficulty we have. What one can do, so can another.

These powers will also say that education is so very important, that people must be taxed to pay for it even if they do not want to be. That is a despotic argument, the kind of thing to which our brightest intellectuals are too much given these days.

These powers will say finally that we do not care enough about education. The answer to that is that we care about it just as the Founders of America did. It is vital to all that is good and true. Therefore it ought not to be left in the hands of people who believe in neither good nor truth. It is too important for that. Let ordinary people decide, place by place and family by family, what is to be done.

This argument cannot be won until it is started. After it is started, it will continue for a long time. Meanwhile, we at Hillsdale College will remember the Founders and continue their work, come what may.

Appendix I

THE NORTHWEST ORDINANCE (1787)
❖ ❖ ❖

BE IT ORDAINED by the authority aforesaid, That there shall be appointed from time to time by Congress, a governor, whose commission shall continue in force for the term of three years, unless sooner revoked by Congress; he shall reside in the district, and have a freehold estate therein in 1,000 acres of land, while in the exercise of his office.

There shall be appointed from time to time by Congress, a secretary, whose commission shall continue in force for four years unless sooner revoked; he shall reside in the district, and have a freehold estate therein in 500 acres of land, while in the exercise of his office. It shall be his duty to keep and preserve the acts and laws passed by the legislature, and the public records of the district, and the proceedings of the governor in his executive department, and transmit authentic copies of such acts and proceedings, every six months, to the Secretary of Congress: There shall also be appointed a court to consist of three judges, any two of whom to form a court, who shall have a common law jurisdiction, and reside in the district, and have each therein a freehold estate in 500 acres of land while in the exercise of their offices; and their commissions shall continue in force during good behavior.

Source: F. N. Thorpe, ed., *Federal and State Constitutions*, vol. 2 (Washington, D.C.: Government Printing Office, 1909), 957.

The governor and judges, or a majority of them, shall adopt and publish in the district such laws of the original States, criminal and civil, as may be necessary and best suited to the circumstances of the district, and report them to Congress from time to time: which laws shall be in force in the district until the organization of the General Assembly therein, unless disapproved of by Congress; but afterwards the Legislature shall have authority to alter them as they shall think fit.

The governor, for the time being, shall be commander-in-chief of the militia, appoint and commission all officers in the same below the rank of general officers; all general officers shall be appointed and commissioned by Congress.

Previous to the organization of the general assembly, the governor shall appoint such magistrates and other civil officers in each county or township, as he shall find necessary for the preservation of the peace and good order in the same: After the general assembly shall be organized, the powers and duties of the magistrates and other civil officers shall be regulated and defined by the said assembly; but all magistrates and other civil officers not herein otherwise directed, shall, during the continuance of this temporary government, be appointed by the governor.

For the prevention of crimes and injuries, the laws to be adopted or made shall have force in all parts of the district, and for the execution of process, criminal and civil, the governor shall make proper divisions thereof; and he shall proceed from time to time as circumstances may require, to lay out the parts of the district in which the Indian titles shall have been extinguished, into counties and townships, subject however to such alterations as may thereafter be made by the legislature.

So soon as there shall be five thousand free male inhabitants of full age in the district, upon giving proof thereof to the governor, they shall receive authority, with time and place, to elect representatives from their counties or townships to represent them in the general assembly:

Provided, That, for every five hundred free male inhabitants, there shall be one representative, and so on progressively with the number of free male inhabitants shall the right of representation increase, until the number of representatives shall amount to twenty-five; after which, the number and proportion of representatives shall be regulated by the legislature:

Provided, That no person be eligible or qualified to act as a representative unless he shall have been a citizen of one of the United States three years, and be a resident in the district, or unless he shall have resided in the district three years; and, in either case, shall likewise hold in his own right, in fee simple, two hundred acres of land within the same;

Provided, also, That a freehold in fifty acres of land in the district, having been a citizen of one of the states, and being resident in the district, or the like freehold and two years residence in the district, shall be necessary to qualify a man as an elector of a representative.

The representatives thus elected, shall serve for the term of two years; and, in case of the death of a representative, or removal from office, the governor shall issue a writ to the county or township for which he was a member, to elect another in his stead, to serve for the residue of the term.

The general assembly or legislature shall consist of the governor, legislative council, and a house of representatives. The Legislative Council shall consist of five members, to continue in office five years, unless sooner removed by Congress; any three of whom to be a quorum: and the members of the Council shall be nominated and appointed in the following manner, to wit: As soon as representatives shall be elected, the Governor shall appoint a time and place for them to meet together; and, when met, they shall nominate ten persons, residents in the district, and each possessed of a freehold in five hundred acres of land, and return their names to Congress; five of whom Congress shall appoint and commission to serve as aforesaid; and, whenever a vacancy shall happen in the council, by death or removal from office, the house of representatives shall nominate two persons, qualified as aforesaid, for each vacancy, and return their names to Congress; one of whom Congress shall appoint and commission for the residue of the term. And every five years, four months at least before the expiration of the time of service of the members of council, the said house shall nominate ten persons, qualified as aforesaid, and return their names to Congress; five of whom Congress shall appoint and commission to serve as members of the council five years, unless sooner removed. And the governor, legislative council, and house of representatives, shall have authority to make laws in all cases, for the good government of the district, not repugnant to the principles and articles in this ordinance established and declared. And all bills, having passed by a majority in the house, and by a majority in the council, shall be referred to the governor for his assent; but no bill, or legislative act whatever, shall be of any force without his assent. The governor shall have power to convene, prorogue, and dissolve the general assembly, when, in his opinion, it shall be expedient.

The governor, judges, legislative council, secretary, and such other officers as Congress shall appoint in the district, shall take an oath or affirmation of fidelity and of office; the governor before the president of congress, and all other officers before the Governor. As soon as a legislature shall be formed in the district, the council and house assembled in one room, shall have authority, by joint ballot, to elect a delegate to Congress, who shall have a seat in Congress, with a right of debating but not of voting during this temporary government.

And, for extending the fundamental principles of civil and religious liberty, which form the basis whereon these republics, their laws and constitutions are erected; to fix and establish those principles as the basis of all laws, constitutions, and governments, which forever hereafter shall be formed in the said territory: to provide also for the establishment of States, and permanent government therein, and for their admission to a share in the federal councils on an equal footing with the original States, at as early periods as may be consistent with the general interest: It is hereby ordained and declared by the authority aforesaid, That the following articles shall be considered as articles of compact between the original States and the people and States in the said territory and forever remain unalterable, unless by common consent, to wit:

ART. 1. No person, demeaning himself in a peaceable and orderly manner, shall ever be molested on account of his mode of worship or religious sentiments, in the said territory.

ART. 2. The inhabitants of the said territory shall always be entitled to the benefits of the writ of habeas corpus, and of the trial by jury; of a proportionate representation of the people in the legislature; and of judicial proceedings according to the course of the common law. All persons shall be bailable, unless for capital offenses, where the proof shall be evident or the presumption great. All fines shall be moderate; and no cruel or unusual punishments shall be inflicted. No man shall be deprived of his liberty or property, but by the judgment of his peers or the law of the land; and, should the public exigencies make it necessary, for the common preservation, to take any person's property, or to demand his particular services, full compensation shall be made for the same. And, in the just preservation of rights and property, it is understood and declared, that no law ought ever to be made, or have force in the said territory, that shall, in any manner whatever, interfere with or affect private contracts or engagements, bona fide, and without fraud, previously formed.

ART. 3. Religion, morality, and knowledge, being necessary to good government and the happiness of mankind, schools and the means of education shall forever be encouraged. The utmost good faith shall always be observed towards the Indians; their lands and property shall never be taken from them without their consent; and, in their property, rights, and liberty, they shall never be invaded or disturbed, unless in just and lawful wars authorized by Congress; but laws founded in justice and humanity, shall from time to time be made for preventing wrongs being done to them, and for preserving peace and friendship with them. . . .

ART. 5. There shall be formed in the said territory, not less than three nor more than five States. . . . And, whenever any of the said States shall have sixty thousand free inhabitants therein, such State shall be admitted, by its delegates, into the Congress of the United States, on an equal footing with the original States in all respects whatever, and shall be at liberty to form a permanent constitution and State government: Provided, the constitution and government so to be formed, shall be republican, and in conformity to the principles contained in these articles; and, so far as it can be consistent with the general interest of the confederacy, such admission shall be allowed at an earlier period, and when there may be a less number of free inhabitants in the State than sixty thousand.

ART. 6. There shall be neither slavery nor involuntary servitude in the said territory, otherwise than in the punishment of crimes whereof the party shall have been duly convicted: Provided, always, That any person escaping into the same, from whom labor or service is lawfully claimed in any one of the original States, such fugitive may be lawfully reclaimed and conveyed to the person claiming his or her labor or service as aforesaid.

Appendix II

HILLSDALE COLLEGE
ARTICLES OF ASSOCIATION (1855)
❖ ❖ ❖

PREAMBLE

WHEREAS the denomination of Christians, known as Free-Will-Baptists, with other friends of education, grateful to God for the inestimable blessings resulting from the prevalence of civil and religious liberty and intelligent piety in the land, and believing that the diffusion of sound learning is essential to the perpetuity of these blessings, having founded and endowed a college at Hillsdale, Hillsdale County, State of Michigan, known and designated by the corporate name of Hillsdale College, which was on the 17th day of May, A.D. 1855, incorporated under the provisions of an Act of the Legislature of said State entitled, "An Act to provide for the incorporation of institutions of learning," approved February 9th, A.D. 1855:

AND WHEREAS the said College has used and exercised the rights, immunities, privileges and franchises granted and conferred by the said statute continually from the date of said incorporation to the present time:

AND WHEREAS the undersigned are desirous of refounding, reestablishing and continuing the said College and to that end have in good faith obtained subscriptions and donations to the amount of over fifty thousand dollars, more than fifty per cent of which has actually been paid in and have elected [names of the 35 Trustees omitted in copying] Trustees:

AND WHEREAS at a special meeting of the Board of Trustees of said College held at Hillsdale, Michigan, on the 26th day of June, A.D. 1891, the

83

said Board of Trustees determined to continue the corporate existence of said College under the statute and directed the several Trustees of said College, heretofore elected and now acting, to make, sign, and execute duplicate Articles of Association for the reorganization and reincorporation of said College and to do all things requisite to retain the said corporate rights, immunities, franchises and property and to continue the corporate existence and work of said College:

NOW THEREFORE, pursuant to the said direction of the Board of Trustees of Hillsdale College, and by virtue of the provisions of Act of the Legislature of said State, entitled, "An Act to provide for the reorganization of corporations or associations for religious, charitable, benevolent or educational purposes, the corporate term if existence of which has heretofore expired or may hereafter expire by limitation, and to fix the duties and liabilities of such renewed corporation or association," approved May 23rd, A.D. 1889, we, the undersigned Trustees, do hereby associate ourselves together and hereby agree to and adopt the foregoing preamble and the following constitution as the Articles of Association for the purpose of reorganization or reincorporation of Hillsdale College under the provisions of an Act of the Legislature of said Legislature of said State entitles, "An act to provide for the incorporation of institutions of learning", approved February 9th, A.D. 1855, as now amended.

CONSTITUTION

Article 1.
The corporate name of this institution shall be Hillsdale College.

Article 2.
The said College shall be continued as heretofore located in Hillsdale, Hillsdale County, in the State of Michigan.

Article 3.
The amount of the capital stock heretofore subscribed, bequeathed, donated and given to said College and now held by it is three hundred and seventeen thousand and three hundred thirty-two and 57/100 dollars, and the amount of such capital stock actually paid is two hundred and eighty-five thousand eight hundred ninety-nine and 96/100 dollars.

Article 4.

The object of this institution is and shall be to furnish to all persons who wish, irrespective of nationality, color or sex, a literary, scientific or theological education as comprehensive and thorough as is usually pursued in other colleges or theological schools in this country, and to combine with this, such moral, social and artistic instruction and culture as will best develop the minds and improve the hearts of the students. The Trustees may from time to time organize additional departments for other branches of education.

Article 5.

The College shall always be under the management and control of thirty-five Trustees who shall be a body corporate and politic, according to the statute aforesaid, elected for the term of five years in such manner that the term of office of seven of the number shall expire annually, but they shall continue in office until their successors shall be elected.

Article 6.

(As amended June 18, 1907)

Religious culture in particular shall be conserved by the College, and by the selection of instructors and other practicable expedients, it shall be a conspicuous aim to teach precept and example the essentials of the Christian faith and religion.

Article 7.

Those several persons who have been duly elected and are now acting as Trustees of said College shall serve out their unexpired terms of office under the new organization, and they are hereby constituted the first Board of Trustees thereof and they and their successors in office shall be the Trustees of Hillsdale College. The names, residences and terms of office of said persons herein constituted the first Board of Trustees under the reorganization of said institution are as follows, to wit:

Article 8.

All vacancies in the Board of Trustees shall be filled by vote of the majority of the Trustees present and voting, by ballot, at any regular meeting.

Article 9.

The Trustees shall meet annually at Hillsdale, Michigan, on the Monday preceding the annual Commencement of the College, but special meetings of the Board shall be called by the Chairman at the same place upon the written request of twelve members of the Board, by giving each Trustee a written notice at least twenty days before such meeting shall be stated, and at any special meeting thirteen members of the Board shall constitute a quorum for the transaction of such business as was specified in the notice of the meeting.

Article 10.

(As Amended June 18, 1907)

These Articles of Association may be amended, at any annual meeting, by a vote of a majority of the Trustees, on the petition of ten members of the Board, written notice of such amendment having been given to each member at least three months previous to such annual meeting.

Article 11.

The president, officers and faculty of Hillsdale College now in office shall continue to hold their several positions and offices during the terms for which they were respectively elected, and the seal of said College now in use and the by-laws now in force are hereby adopted and shall be continued in use and in force until changed by proper authority.

Article 12.

All the rights, privileges, immunities, franchises and property of every kind, now held, possessed or owned by Hillsdale College, shall, by the execution and filing of this instrument, be transferred and assigned to and be forever vested in Hillsdale College as reorganized and reincorporated by these presents, pursuant to the statutes of this state.

IN WITNESS WHEREOF and for the purpose of organizing ourselves into a body corporate we have severally subscribed the forgoing Articles of Association this 26th day of June, A.D. 1891. [Names of 35 subscribing Trustees omitted in copying.]

Appendix III

THE COLLEGE AND THE REPUBLIC

EDMUND B. FAIRFIELD
PRESIDENT, HILLSDALE COLLEGE
❖ ❖ ❖

*Remarks Given Upon the Laying of the Cornerstone
of the New College Building at Hillsdale, July 4, 1853*

Printed in the Hillsdale Standard, *May 8, 1855*

MR. PRESIDENT AND FELLOW CITIZENS:
I must confess to the reluctance which I have felt in consenting to occupy your attention at this hour as well as during the next. But circumstances, and your committee of arrangements, have imposed upon me the necessity, to which I submit.

But I may also as well acknowledge that my embarrassment finds no little relief in seeing before me so large a gathering of the citizens of the County at large, with whom it has been my privilege to form a most agreeable acquaintance in connection with the enterprise which has called us to this spot today. The cordiality, the unanimity and the liberality with which they have contributed to the erection of the building whose cornerstone is now to be laid, have not often been paralleled in the history of such institutions. And we have before us in this immense concourse of people, from all parts of the County, only another manifestation of the same spirit and of the same lively interest which has from the first pervaded this whole movement.

Fellow citizens—it were a vain thing for me to say that you have the cordial thanks of the trustees and officers of the College for what you have done, and are still doing in its behalf. This you know full well. And what is more, you have already given yourselves a hearty vote of thanks for the interest you have taken in this work; and your presence and countenances today assure us that you are not yet ready to reconsider that vote. It is not merely the money which you have furnished and engaged to furnish for this work, but the cordial goodwill with which it has been done, that has cheered us on.

The law of custom imposes upon me the duty of saying a few things appropriate to the occasion. That duty I shall aim to discharge to the best of my ability, only premising that however deficient my words shall be in other respects, they shall not be wanting in brevity.

There are many suitable topics that naturally suggest themselves; but, convened as we are, to lay the cornerstone or a College edifice on this anniversary of our national independence, none presents itself to my mind more naturally than this: The Connection Between our Republican and our Educational Institutions. This, then is my text for a few brief utterances. The history of Liberty has been the history of Intelligence. "The fathers" brought with them to this goodly land the Common School and the College. These had prepared the way for rational civil and religious liberty, and they were ever to stand as its reliable fortifications. Ignorance is rightly deemed an essential prerequisite to slavery. The more the ignorance, the better the slave, and when the bondman becomes possessed of intelligence, his oppressor will tell you that the devil is in him. Too much intelligence is the worst devil that oppression knows. The process of education is continually cherishing an independence of thought that is in close alliance with civil liberty. Give freedom to mind and you will not easily put chains upon the body. Education gives to each man an individual personality that well enough prepares him to be a freeman, but sadly disqualifies him from being a slave. It is a continual process of *self cultivation*: introducing him into the hidden arena of his own intellectual nature, making him acquainted with his own powers and capacities. Whatever else he may study—whether the heavens above him, or the earth beneath him, or the world around him, there is continually a reflection of himself, and he who knows himself, knows that he was not made to be a slave; and the next thing he knows, is that no human arm is strong enough to make him one. The victim of despotic oppression must as far as possible be stripped of all consciousness of personality: he must be hidden from himself; his noble nature must be unseen by his own eyes, that he may be content to be a thing—that he may be stupidly submissive when the tyrant oppressor despoils him of his rights and crushes out of him his soul. Our educational institutions furnish a poor reparation for such a despotic rule. Intelligence, at the same time that it prepares a man for the enjoyment of his liberty, cultivates a sad distaste for the sweets of slavery. The man who knows not what he is or what he was made to be, may tacitly consent to be a mere appendage to another; but as process of intellectual development goes on, he discovers in himself the equal of his lord; he has revealed to him the fundamental doctrine of human equality, and he can no longer consent to be but the fraction of a unit. He sees in himself a WHOLE MAN, and in another he sees no more. He recognizes in himself a separate responsible agent; and as said Webster, "The greatest thought of my life is that of my individual responsibility to God." So with every man. And when once inspired with such a thought as this, he is forever above that level where the tyrant may find a facile subject. The self-respect which such a man feels, and cannot but feel, illy qualifies him for the place of a menial, or to do the bidding of a haughty lord: he respects other men as men, and himself as a man too, and he thinks too highly of his manhood to consent to lose it, or allow it to be absorbed in that of another.

But Educational Institutions are not only invaluable in preparing for the enjoyment of rational liberty, but they are equally so in perpetuating it; they are the constant allies and the eternal bulwarks of all the institutions of Republicanism. No nation approaching the confines of civilization but deems it important to educate their princes. The heir of sovereignty must be qualified to meet the responsibilities of their kingly office. In a Republic the people are the kings. I speak today to those who either are, or are to be, the sovereigns of the land. You are not merely law makers, but make those that are law makers. If you wear not the insignia of an aristocratic nobility—in the shape of ribbons, red and green and blue—you may remember that the inhabitants of Lilliput did and you are not over-anxious to imitate the little six-inch men of the far-famed land. The insights of nature's nobility are the hand-hardened by toil, and the face radiant with intelligence and manly virtue.

You, fellow citizens, are not merely dukes and lords, and barons and knights; but kings, and sons of kings, and the fathers of kings. The crowns that come to you from the heads of those that lie low in the grave, will soon rest upon the heads of these *princes of the blood* whom I see before me. It is for the fathers to see that the sons are qualified for the responsibilities of American citizenship, and it is for the sons to see to it that they do not dishonor the crowns, the crowns that the Republic has placed upon their heads. The elements of power and stability in a nation of freemen are the intelligence and virtue of the people who bear rule.

What constitutes a State?
Not high-raised battlement, or labored mound.
Thick wall, or moated gate:
Not cities proud with spires and turrets crown'd,
Not bays and broad-armed ports,
Where laughing at the storm, rich navies ride:
Not starred and spangled court,
Where low-brow'd baseness wafts perfume to pride;
No: Men, high-minded Men,
With powers as far above dull brutes endued,
In forest, brake or den;
As beasts excel cold rocks and bramble rude,
Men who their duties know,
But know their rights, and knowing dare maintain;
Prevent the long-aimed blow,
And crush the tyrant while they rend the chain,
These Constitute a State.

If there is in a Republican government a *power behind the throne*, that power is to be found in public sentiment. And in the formation of public sentiment, our Educational institutions exert an influence beyond the power of computation. Happily for the interests of liberty and Republicanism, Colleges have almost universally ranged themselves on the side of popular rights. In every contest between the prerogatives of the ruler and the rights of the ruled, they have defended the right against the might.

Again: the strength of a Republican government is to be found not so much in the rigid enforcement by arms of the laws of the Senate, as in the fact that these laws are self-imposed by the intelligent perception on the part of the people of their wisdom and of their necessity. Let the law be written not merely upon the statute book, but upon the hearts and minds of intelligent citizens, and the willing homage which they pay to its mandates is liberty itself in the highest form and truest type; while the constrained obedience rendered only at the point of the bayonet, even to wise and necessary laws, is little else than slavery. The one is Republican-ism; the other is Despotism. The one is Liberty, regulated by intelligence; the other is the recklessness of ignorance and the restlessness of insub-ordination, restrained by force. Not long can a Republic maintain its ex-istence as such without at least that measure of general intelligence that perceives and acknowledges the necessity of just laws, and that for the public good yields a cheerful and unconstrained obedience to them.

Unrestrained freedom is anarchy. Restrained only by force and arms, is despotism; self-restrained is Republicanism. Wherever there is want-ing the intelligence and virtue requisite for the latter, Republicanism ex-pires. The complicated machinery of free institutions must have an adequate regulator; and that is to be found in an enlightened public con-science. This our Educational institutions—teaching as well the laws of social morality as of physical science—are omnipotent in forming. And as we cherish the heritage of civil and religious liberty which has come down to us, so it becomes us to cherish the College, the Academy and the Common School, permeated by Christian influence, which alone have secured us this inheritance, prepared us for enjoying and appreciate it, or can prove its efficient conservators.

But more than this: our Educational Institutions are eminently Republican in their very nature. Here are brought together the sons of wealth and of poverty, of patrician and plebian descent, to meet upon the same arena, to wrestle in the same intellectual gymnasium, run in the same race, and contend for the same honors, upon equal terms, and with equal chances of success, only as the gifts of nature, or the vigorous industry, the close application, or the determined perseverance of each individual can-didate shall vary the equation; and this variation, justice requires us to say, is often in favor of the inheritor of poverty and toil, rather than of riches and titles. Within College walls aristocratic dignities, aristocratic pretensions, or aristocratic airs, avail their possessor but little. Woe to the luckless youth that puts them on. Here, if nowhere else, the mind is the measure of the man. Long genealogies and endless pedigrees are a sorry offset for short memories and shallow brains. Here is valued not so much the crown as the head that wears it. Lace, and ribbons, and purple and fine linens, are a poor compensation for a deficient cranium. Nor does a full purse make amends for an empty head. Gold is not legal tender for College honors. A soft hand is no passport for a soft head. The sun-burnt farmer's boy, with his inheritance of poverty, hardships and toil, stands side by side with the fair-browed youth who is heir of millions, and who eats the bread of another's sweat; only that like Saul among his fellows, he is not unfrequently higher than any of the sons of wealth and luxury, from his shoulders *and upward*. For an illustration of true Republicanism, give us such a community as is found at the Common School and the College, and you may and a better if you can. And the Republic owes it to itself to open wide to all its sons the doors of the Common School, the Academy, and the College. She has an interest in her children that a monarch can never have. Her life is identified with theirs. They constitute the essential parts of her own vital organism; and such and so many are the sympathies of this complicated and living machinery, that if one member suffer, all the members suffer with it. She may so rear her sons, that they shall be her honor and her ornament not only, but her strength and her support: too, on the other hand, she may, by a criminal recklessness, not only lose the strength and the glory which they might impart to her, but virtually train them to inflict upon her the bitterest curses, and in the end prove her remediless destruction.

No nation, but least of all a Republic, can afford to lose from her garden of beauty and her crown of glory, those of whom the Poet has so pensively sung:

> Full many a flower is born to blush unseen,
> And waste its fragrance on the desert air;
> Full many a gem of purest ray serene,
> The dark unfathom'd caves of ocean bear.

Still less can she long survive the suicidal policy of so abandoning her children to ignorance and to vice that they shall not only be ciphers in the account, but positive factors, whose product is gangrene and death.

The College is the friend of the Republic, and the Republic should be the friend of the College. Our Educational establishments ever have been the faithful allies and firm supporters of all that is ennobling in our free institutions, and every layer of the Republic should see to it that they are nurtured and guarded with a sleepless vigilance.

Let it be deemed no sacrilege, therefore, that we are convened upon this day, sacred to liberty, to human rights, and to patriotism, to lay the cornerstone of this College edifice. I deem it an auspicious coincidence. May it prove a significant prophecy upon this anniversary of the day on which our fathers laid the foundations of the beautiful temple of our National Liberties, we come to lay the cornerstone of this spacious temple of Science. May the walls reared upon this foundation, stand for ages to come, sacred as well to freedom, humanity, philanthropy and true patriotism, as to sound science pure morality, and true religion. The cornerstone will now be laid.

Appendix IV

TRUTH AND ERROR

FREDERICK DOUGLASS

❖ ❖ ❖

Speech given at Hillsdale College, January 1863
Douglass Monthly, *February* 1863
Account from the Chicago Tribune

DOUGLASS REMARKED that our government had discovered a new truth, and was organizing it into law. He could only talk of old truths—Properly speaking, there was no such thing as new truth. Error might be old or new; but truth was as old as the universe, based upon a sure foundation, and could not be overthrown.

Truth was a unit; error was multitudinous. While man had but one chance of hitting the right path, he had many chances of falling into error. The world held out very many false lights, to lure mankind from the true path. The wonder was not that men erred, but that no such advancement had been made in important truth.

Truth was powerful; a single individual, armed with truth, was a majority against the world. Thirty years ago, Wm. Lloyd Garrison advocated a bold truth. He was a majority then, as truly as he is now. He said that slaveholders were a bad set of fellows. The people hardly believed him then; but they believed him now, for besides his testimony they had that of the slaveholders themselves.

Truth was always safe; error was always dangerous. Why was it, the speaker inquired, that our once peaceful country was now filled with contention and reddened with blood? It was because we had tolerated and nourished a stupendous wrong—the wrong of human slavery. It was no strange event that had happened to our country. It was but the logical sequence of the exciting cause alluded to.

A certain great man had said that it was useless to reenact the laws of God. But a still greater man had declared that it was useless to reenact any other than the laws of God. We had attempted to contravene the laws of God by transforming men into beasts of burden. Some people did not like progress. The old Hunkers did not like it. There were some towns which, it was said, were entirely finished, and would not be in the least injured by being fenced in. The same was true of certain individuals, they were *done for*. They were started out of their sense at the promulgation of what was to them a new truth; or the new application of an old truth. They were in favor of the world as it used to be; the union as it was, but in favor of nothing as it ought to be.

Certain newspapers had recently been focusing upon Boston, because its citizens had once persecuted women accused of witchcraft. But such papers were only using such things to justify their own pet principles of women-whipping and man stealing. Boston had progressed, but these old Hunkers had now begun where Boston left off.

Error was always afraid of truth; hence it went armed with bludgeons and the instruments of brute force. Bully Brooks walked into the Senate chamber and stuck down Sumner, but he left the Senator's argument standing. But that was the best Brooks could do, for he was on the side of the cudgel and the brickbat, and had no other arguments that he could use. Yet that argument of Charles Sumner would stand forever, and inspire the hearts of the people for years after slavery had passed away.

This war was the legitimate result of slavery. That iniquitous institution had been treated with the most profound respect, even by the people of the free North. It had been regarded as a sacred institution, which could not be touched, or even discussed. The Abolitionists were often charged with bringing on the war. But of all classes of persons in the nation, they were the least obnoxious to such a charge. Had the opponents of slavery been allowed the right of free speech—as the Federal Constitution declared every American citizen should have—the enormities of the "patriarchal institution" would have been exposed, and in due time it might have done away with in a peaceful manner. But no such right had been allowed. The votaries of it had been loud in their advocacy of slavery; its opponents had been repeatedly gagged and driven from Southern soil, whenever they opened their mouths against the property in man.

A fatal blow had at last been struck at the root of the gigantic evil. The President's proclamation had given the slaves the *legal* right to liberty. Now they could obtain their personal freedom without trampling upon civil laws. Instead of rising up as insurrectionists, in opposition to law, they could rise up in obedience to law. It was a proud thought that the first man to put the knife of military power to the throat of this vile monster, was an Illinoisan.

At last the edict of freedom had gone forth, and the people were prepared to sustain it and carry it out. The speaker had a great deal of confidence in the virtue of the North, but still more in the villainy of the South. He thanked Abe Lincoln for what he had done towards destroying slavery, and he also felt grateful to Jeff Davis.

One of the most hopeful indications of the war was a proposition before Congress to raise 150,000 black troops. We had been fighting the rebellion with only one hand—fighting it with our soft delicate white hand, while the hard, black hand had been tied behind our back. That hand must be unloosed, if we knock down the rebellion.

But it had been said that the Negroes would not fight. Who believed it? These same Hunkers also declared that the Negroes of the South would cut their masters' throats and run away. We were told that they would not work; and then in the next breath the same croakers declared that if set free they would come up North and take away all the employment from our laboring population! The trust was, the slaves would both fight and work, if by doing so they could obtain their freedom and earn an honest livelihood. They were the only real Union men in the South. Now they were beginning to feel that their long-looked for day of deliverance had come, or at least was within their reach.

The speaker would up his address with a very interesting recital of the grand jubilee which was held in Boston on the first day of January, in which he was a participant. At the close of his remarks, Mr. Douglass was greeted with rounds of applause, as indeed he had often been during the entire lecture.... — *Chicago Tribune*

Appendix V

HILLSDALE COLLEGE
DECLARATION OF INDEPENDENCE
ADOPTED FEBRUARY 16, 1962
REAFFIRMED JUNE 3, 1966
❖ ❖ ❖

WHEREAS, Hillsdale College was conceived as an independent educational institution and dedicated to an educational philosophy embracing America's basic ideals; and

WHEREAS, since 1844 it has remained steadfastly faithful to these concepts; and

WHEREAS, the thousands of young men and young women who have studied here have been taught some fundamental truths; among these is that the freedom guaranteed them as citizens of this great country is the freedom to dream and aspire without limit and the freedom to fulfill their dreams and aspirations without interference; that our country's greatness is the result not of government benevolence but rather of individual initiative and enterprise; that responsibility is the counterpart of independence; and

WHEREAS, we hold these views to be as valid today as they were in 1844 despite the appearance and growth of a contrary philosophy based on government paternalism; and

WHEREAS, it is our conviction that this contrary philosophy is negatory to the traditional beliefs and teachings of Hillsdale College and is to be deplored as harmful to the continued development of our country both morally and economically; Now

99

THEREFORE, BE IT RESOLVED, That it be the decision of the Board of Trustees of Hillsdale College to reaffirm its historic independence and to resist subsidization of its affairs by the Federal government. Acknowledging that the possibility of failure is a concomitant of independence, the Trustees place their trust in God and in the dedication and generosity of students, alumni and friends who share their views. With this help, and through their own continuing efforts, they are confident that the principles to which the College is dedicated will continue to be available to young men and young women seeking independent higher education.

Appendix VI

OUR RESPONSIBILITY TO AMERICA

LARRY P. ARNN
PRESIDENT, HILLSDALE COLLEGE
❖ ❖ ❖

From a speech delivered on October 3, 2002, at the Broadmoor Hotel and Resort in Colorado Springs, Colorado, at the twentieth anniversary conference of the Hillsdale National Leadership Seminar.

We meet here to celebrate the twentieth anniversary of these National Leadership seminars. Begun by my predecessor George Roche III in 1982, these conferences have played a powerful part in the recent history of our College. Many of you here know how much fun they can be. You know also that they can be inspiring. They have lasted a long time for a reason.

Part of the cause of their success has to do with the subject matter they cover—the great affairs of the American nation. They have ranged widely across national and world affairs, across tax policy and defense; regulation and business; family and education; schools and churches. The topics seem at first diverse, but in fact they concern a central theme. I want to talk about that theme today.

To see this theme, we have to think a little about our country and the crisis it faces. We have to think about Hillsdale College, and about the relation between the country and the College. That relation has changed during the last 30 years from what it was in the first 30 years of the history of the College. This is not because the College has changed, but because the country has changed. In that change can be found the key to our situation today and what we are to do about it.

First, let us look at America. Right now it is engaged in a great battle. It is not only the obvious and urgent battle with terrorism, but also a battle over the meaning of the country itself. This battle concerns certain key words that have ever been identified with our nation. Words—ideas and principles—are at the heart of our nation. Over the course of history, our geography has changed massively. Our population has grown manyfold, and as at the beginning we are a nation of immigrants and their children. Yet somehow America has a definite meaning, a meaning in principle that can be measured in practice.

We can see the meaning in the fact that we have a national birthday. Ask yourself, what is the birthday of France? Or China? Or England? One day every summer we celebrate the making of our country. As John Adams predicted, this day is the anniversary of a document that states the purposes of our nation. Abraham Lincoln once spoke of a "central idea" in America, from which all of our "minor thoughts radiate." The Declaration of Independence called this idea a "self-evident truth." It is the idea that each of us is equally a child of God, born the same kind of creature, and so equal with respect to our rights.

We have these key terms—rights, equality, liberty. And at certain times in our history we have a pivotal debate about what these terms mean. The political party commanding a majority has changed but a few times in our history, each time after such a debate. At Hillsdale College we like to say that "ideas have consequences." These are the ideas that have the most profound consequences.

These words do not refer merely to theories, detached from how we live and act and think. These ideas live in our hearts, and grow up with us in our homes and families. Americans are, after all, a distinctive people. They start businesses more often than other people do. They give to charity more often than other people do. They think, or they have thought, that their own families and their own neighborhoods, their own businesses and their communities, are their own things to direct and to nurture. They do not look to others to tell them how to manage their own affairs. They know how to compete with each other and cooperate with each other at the same time, energetically and with good will. They prefer doing things of their own volition and by themselves. They do not like war, but when they are compelled to fight they make good warriors for the same reason that they make good businesspeople or good neighbors, and they can be ruthless. This is the American character.

That is the old idea of America. Now there is a new idea. According to it, human nature is not fixed but evolves. Furthermore, this evolution comes to be something that we ourselves control. To believe that man can control his evolution is to believe in effect that we can create ourselves. We can take the place of God. This way of thinking comes to us from German historicism, but in America it became known as progressivism. Early in the last century it began to take over the academic world. Gradually it took over the Democratic Party and got a very powerful influence on the government.

These ideas, too, are not just theories, debated in the ivory tower. Hillary Clinton gave a commencement speech at the University of Texas in April of 1993. *The New York Times Magazine* reported that because she wrote this speech so soon after the death of her father, she used it to pour out her innermost feelings. The central point of this speech is the need to "redefine who we are as human beings in this post-modern age," something that requires "remolding society" and "reinventing our institutions." And of course the engine of all this change is government.

Compare this with the doctrine in the Declaration of Independence that human beings have a certain nature, that they may be governed only in a certain way, and that whatever the location or period of history, any government that does not govern people in that way is wrong.

Just as the old understanding of government implied a certain kind of Constitution and way of life, so the new understanding implies a different kind of Constitution and way of life. Today, the Constitution hardly functions at all as a limit on the actions of the federal government. We citizens expect different things from the government, and tolerate actions by it that would have outraged our fathers. Think, for example, what has become of our property rights. The Founders saw property rights as a sort of summary of all our rights. Where the right to property is protected, entrepreneurship flourishes, and people are able to care for themselves.

If it is not protected, then for the same reason freedom of speech and worship and equality of justice will suffer, too.

In 1944, Franklin Roosevelt gave a speech about a "new bill of rights," founded upon "new self-evident truths." Notice the use of the language of the Declaration, but now put to a new purpose. One of these new rights is that a farmer should be guaranteed a price for his crops. This is the idea that has produced the mohair subsidy and the annual payments to farming corporations. Roosevelt presents this as an extension of the old rights protected in our Constitution, but in fact it is the abnegation of those rights. It inspires a battle in society over who gets what from the government, or rather, from the taxpayer. The easy path to wealth is to become a member of a protected class. The distortions this breeds in the economy are massive, and they grow steadily. Whereas the old idea of rights—that they can only include things that do not take from another—breeds harmony in society, so the new idea breeds conflict.

The same thing is happening in the political system. Because we have the first purely representative government ever built, we must rely entirely upon elections to control the government. Today elections are managed ever more tightly, and notoriously, with a purpose to affect who wins. In the last two months, federal regulators ruled that Jay Leno and David Letterman will not violate election law if they joke about candidates just prior to an election. But of course a government that can rule that this is legal, may soon rule that it is not. Meanwhile, electoral issues move steadily into the courts, where lawyers and judges may decide who can run and who will win. Just recently the New Jersey Supreme Court, the same court that ruled that the Boy Scouts of America may not exclude homosexual scoutmasters, permitted a party to substitute a popular candidate for an unpopular one, after the statutory time limit had expired. If this continues, elections will become like relay races at a track meet.

I will mention later federal education policy, which now dictates to almost every college in the land about the most minor details. It has developed in just the same way as most of the other interminable intrusions of the federal administrative system into things that were previously private or local.

How does this new understanding affect our national character? Have you noticed that we are not as apt as we used to be to take care of our families for ourselves? Have you noticed that we are not as apt as we used to be to resent subsidy of ourselves by the government? Have you noticed that we are not as apt as we used to be to think that there is a standard of uprightness to which we are to conform? Ride the back roads across America and notice how many buildings have been built to house federal bureaucracies. In the 30 years since *Imprimis* was founded, the U.S. economy has grown in real terms two-and-one-half times, while the federal government has grown eight times.

What do we do about this? The answer can be found in the history of our College.

Hillsdale College was founded in 1844, 16 years before the Civil War. Its leaders then were Ransom Dunn, Edmund Fairfield, and Austin Blair. Like the nation, the College began with a clear statement of principle, a principle stated in our founding document. It begins with a sentence that echoes the great documents of our nation's founding. It expresses gratitude to "God for the prevalence in the land of the inestimable blessings of civil and religious freedom and intelligent piety." In order to preserve these blessings, "sound learning" is necessary. That, say our founders, is why they established Hillsdale College. If you learn, you can have these blessings. If you are ignorant, you cannot.

One of our founders, Ransom Dunn, probably the greatest man ever to work at our College, was a member of our faculty for 50 years. One of his sons died in the Civil War in the arms of another. At one point, because we needed money, Dunn got on a horse, rode out and raised it, five dollars at a time, from farmers and merchants across the Midwest. He was gone for two years and came back with $10,000, a huge sum. This was a great act of faith on his part, and on the part of those who gave money. They believed that by supporting liberal education, they were making America fit to be free.

Pursuing this end, Hillsdale College quickly became one of the most influential small colleges in the land. October 2004 will mark the 150th anniversary of the first Republican Convention. Abraham Lincoln was a friend of many people who worked at our College at that time, and the chairman of the first Republican Convention was Austin Blair, a member of our faculty. Frederick Douglass spoke on our campus, as did Edward Everett, the man who preceded Lincoln at Gettysburg. And more of our boys fought for the Union in the Civil War than any non-military college that we can find. Ideas, the ideas that one learns through liberal education, had consequences. Although the College was small, its consequences spread across an entire nation.

Hillsdale had a devotion to the nation that was open and emphatic. The campus as it now exists was dedicated on the Fourth of July in 1853. The speech by Edmund Fairfield appealed to the good of America, to freedom, to service to God, and to the necessity of education to all of them.

Consider now the modern history of Hillsdale College. In our first 30 years, we were fighting to save the Union. For the last 30 years, we have been fighting to keep the federal government out of our business. This fight actually started in the late 1950s, when the federal government decided to subsidize education. The leaders of Hillsdale believed that this federal subsidy was not constitutional. They also thought that it would distort liberal arts education. And so our College refused all that money. J. Donald Phillips was president then, and in 1966 he issued the Hillsdale College Declaration of Independence, a noble document that makes excellent reading still today.

In 1971, George Roche became president, and in 1975 the College got a letter from the U.S. Department of Education. It said that some of our kids were getting student aid—such as the G.I. Bill—from the federal government. It said that for Hillsdale to accept such students, it had to become a signatory to Title IV of the Higher Education Act. When I first came to the College, I ordered up a copy of Title IV. I started reading it, and after a few pages I decided that I am either not intelligent enough, or (I hope) too intelligent, to read it. So I ordered the kit that one uses to sign up for Title IV, and the kit was very understandable. To become a signatory, several people in the College would have to sign statements of personal liability to comply with Title IV, which is now almost 500 pages long. This would mean that the administration would have to do what federal regulators tell us, rather than what our board of trustees or our mission statement tells us.

Title IV says, among other things, that colleges must count their students and staff by the color of their skin. And as I mentioned, we had boys fight and die in the Civil War in opposition to just that. I told somebody in the Michigan Department of Education one time, "You came down here with a clipboard and walked around campus counting people by their color. This is an embarrassing thing to do, and you know it. I want you to know that we have spilled blood on the ground over that principle. We will not be made to violate it."

The first thing that President Roche and the Board of Trustees did when they received this ultimatum from the federal government was to sue. In 1984, the U.S. Supreme Court decided against Hillsdale nine to nothing. Along with Chairman Don Mossey and the Board, President Roche decided to give up the federal student aid money. George Roche was, for 28 years as president, a brave and a firm man in commitment to Hillsdale's principles. When he embarked on the effort to keep the College independent of federal control, neither he nor the Board had any way to be sure they could find the money. Just like the founders of the College, they acted in faith that they were right and that a way would be found. It was a shining moment. Neither that moment nor the people who made it possible will be forgotten so long as our College stands.

Of course those who have fought this battle for Hillsdale College have won splendid results so far. The money we need to make up for the federal aid has increased by a factor of 15 since those first days. But we have been able to find it. We have been holding these conferences for 20 years, and they continue to be well attended by people like yourselves, people who love their country and wish to join together to put it right. We have been publishing *Imprimis* for 30 years. It has grown in circulation from 1,500 to more than 1,100,000; it has more than 150,000 additional readers since I came to the College. Just as in its early days, little Hillsdale College is a beacon to the nation.

Hillsdale was a patriotic college in 1980, just as it was in 1850. It holds to the same principles today, but now it is in conflict with the very thing it had fought before to preserve. This carries a lesson for every American.

In the beginning, certain ideas were powerful in shaping our nation and forming its character. At key moments in our history, these ideas have been controversial. Their meaning has been debated and the future has been shaped by the course of these debates. Today the meaning of these terms has been claimed for a new cause, a cause contradictory to their first meaning.

Education has always been important in these debates. In a nation of ideas, it matters decisively what is thought, especially by those who teach the young, especially those among the young who are likely to become leaders. For instance, if young people go to college with the understanding that they have a right to go, and therefore that someone else is obliged to pay for it, they learn a lesson about the meaning of rights. If they go to a college where their scholarships and loans are provided by private citizens, who give their money voluntarily, and if they are asked to write thank you letters to those benefactors, they learn something else.

We have big government today because of a vain attempt to replace the authority of the "laws of nature and of nature's God" with the authority of lawmakers—no, with the authority of regulators. We will turn back from that attempt, or we will lose the ability to exercise our rights and control our government.

Woodrow Wilson, a leading figure in progressivism, called our Declaration of Independence "obsolete." But he, like Franklin Roosevelt and more recently the Clintons, understood the power of its terms. They used those terms for new purposes. They altered their meaning, and by that means, over two generations, revolutionized the constitutional system.

It is an important fact that the debate they began has not yet been completed. Though the aims of the progressive movement have been far advanced, they have not been fully won. Their advocates have fought a long battle with the conservative forces in the land, among whom Hillsdale College has been proudly ranked for over 30 years. Thus the American people still live for the most part in love of liberty, in vigorous enterprise, in respect for God, in devotion to the common-sense understanding of right and wrong. Osama bin Laden is the latest in a line of tyrants to believe that our soul has been corrupted and when attacked we will run away. Like those before him, he has learned that we are a people in whom courage, and all the other virtues too, still thrive.

If then we are not to despair, we should learn the lessons of the past. To keep our freedom, we must study with renewed diligence the principles that make it right. We should learn again to use the tools bequeathed to us. We should talk and act like Americans, loving our country, respecting that Providence upon whom our Fathers called, and keeping faith in the Right, as God gives us to see it.

The history of Hillsdale College is in fact nothing other or less than the telling, on a smaller scale, of the history of our nation. Because we have held fast to the faith of our original creed, we have been in conflict now for a long time with the government that we have also fought bravely, at every time of need, to preserve. We are not given other tools than study and learning, prayer and devotion, argument and action, with which to defend our liberty. If a little College can stand for that through war and trial, anyone can do it.

There is the hope. There is the method. We at Hillsdale College will abandon neither.

Appendix VII

HILLSDALE BOARD RESOLUTION

PASSED BY THE HILLSDALE COLLEGE BOARD OF TRUSTEES
OCTOBER 17, 2003

❖ ❖ ❖

WHEREAS the Board of Trustees and Administration of Hillsdale College have been entrusted with, and are determined to uphold, the original and great principles and mission of the College as set down nearly 160 years ago by its founders; and

WHEREAS those principles and that mission require the College to provide "sound learning" to all willing students, and to do so in a way that perpetuates the "blessings of civil and religious liberty" and "intelligent piety" in the land; and

WHEREAS the entanglement of the federal government in the financing of colleges and universities, and the consequent regulation of these institutions by federal agencies, violate the idea of limited government embodied in the Constitution; and

WHEREAS such violations are inherently corrupt, as seen in attempts of the Department of Education to force Hillsdale College to count its students by race, in direct violation of the noblest principles of the College and of America; now therefore be it

RESOLVED that Hillsdale College will continue zealously to defend and uphold, against all threats and inducements, its independence from federal government financing and federal government regulation; and be it further

---

This resolution was published on a full page of *The New York Times* on December 5, 2003.

RESOLVED that the Administration of Hillsdale College, with the support of the Board of Trustees, will continue to provide not only the finest liberal arts education, but also national leadership in promoting the principles of liberty across the land, and it will pursue these aims in strict avoidance of all subsidy from the federal taxpayer.

SELECTED BIBLIOGRAPHY
❖ ❖ ❖

Barnett, Randy E. "The Original Meaning of the Necessary and Proper Clause." *University of Pennsylvania Journal of Constitutional Law* 6 (October 2003): 183–220.

Church, Robert L., and Michael W. Sedlak. *Education in the United States: An Interpretive History*. New York: The Free Press, 1976.

Cohen, Sheldon S. *A History of Colonial Education, 1607–1776*. New York: John Wiley & Sons, 1974.

Conant, James B. *Thomas Jefferson and the Development of American Public Education*. Berkeley: University of California Press, 1962.

Cremin, Lawrence A. *Traditions of American Education*. New York: Basic Books: 1977.

_____. *American Education: The National Experience, 1783–1876*. New York: Harper & Row, 1980.

Deutsch, Kenneth L., and John A. Murley, eds. *Leo Strauss, the Straussians, and the American Regime*. Lanham, MD: Rowman & Littlefield, 1999.

De Tocqueville, Alexis. *Democracy in America*. Translated and edited by Harvey C. Mansfield and Delba Winthrop. Chicago: University of Chicago Press, 2000.

French, William M. *America's Educational Tradition: An Interpretive History*. Boston: D.C. Heath & Company, 1964.

Geiger, Roger L. *To Advance Knowledge: The Growth of American Research Universities, 1900–1940*. New York: Oxford University Press, 1986.

Gilbert, Arlan K. *Historic Hillsdale College: Pioneer in Higher Education, 1844–1900*. Hillsdale, MI: Hillsdale College Press, 1991.

_____. *Hillsdale Honor: The Civil War Experience*. Hillsdale, MI: Hillsdale College Press, 1994.

_____. *The Permanent Things:Hillsdale College, 1900–1994*. Hillsdale, MI: Hillsdale College Press, 1998.

Good, H. G. *A History of American Education*. 2nd ed. New York: The Macmillan Company, 1962.

Gross, Richard E. *Heritage of American Education*. Boston: Allyn and Bacon, 1962.

Hamilton, Alexander, James Madison, and John Jay. *The Federalist Papers*. Edited by Clinton Rossiter, with an introduction and notes by Charles R. Kesler. New York: Mentor, 2003.

Higher Education Act of 1965, Public Law 89-329, 79 STAT 1219, November 8, 1965.

Knight, Edgar W. *Education in the United States*. 3rd ed. New York: Greenwood Press, 1951.

Knight, Edgar W., and Clifton L. Hall, eds. *Readings in American Educational History*. New York: Appleton-Century-Crofts, 1951.

Krason, Stephen M. *The Recovery of American Education: Reclaiming a Vision*. Lanham, MD: University Press of America, 1991.

Lord, Carnes. *Education and Culture in the Political Thought of Aristotle*. Ithaca, NY: Cornell University Press, 1982.

Marini, John. *The Politics of Budget Control: Congress, the Presidency, and the Growth of the Administrative State*. Washington, D.C.: Crane Russak, 1992.

Meyer, Adolphe E. *An Educational History of the American People*. New York: McGraw-Hill, 1957.

Morrish, Ivor. *Education Since 1800*. New York: Barnes & Noble, 1970.

Nie, Norman H., Jane Junn, and Kenneth Stehlik-Barry. *Education and Democratic Citizenship in America*. Chicago: University of Chicago Press, 1996.

Pulliam, John D. *History of Education in America*. Columbus, OH: Charles E. Merril Publishing Company, 1968.

Rickover, H. G. *Education and Freedom*. New York: E. P. Dutton & Co., 1959.

Rudolph, Frederick, ed. *Essays on Education in the Early Republic*. Cambridge: Harvard University Press, Belknap Press,1965.

Schaefer, William D. *Education Without Compromise: From Chaos to Coherence in Higher Education*. San Francisco: Jossey-Bass Publishers, 1990.

Sharpes, Donald K. *Education and the U.S. Government*. New York: St. Martin's Press, 1987.

Sloan, Douglas, ed. *The Great Awakening and Education: A Documentary History*. New York: Teachers College Press, 1973.

Veysey, Laurence R. *The Emergence of the American University*. Chicago: University of Chicago Press, 1965.

Warren, Donald R. *To Enforce Education: A History of the Founding Years of the United States Office of Education*. Detroit: Wayne State University Press, 1974.

Wills, Garry. *Mr. Jefferson's University*. Washington, D.C.: The National Geographic Society, 2002.

INDEX

❖ ❖ ❖

Northwest Ordinance (1787), 2–7, 13, 19, 74, 77–82
Northwest Territory, 2, 3

O

Office of Civil Rights, 50, 51
Office of Education, 34
"Our Responsibility to America" (Larry P. Arnn), 101–9

P

Percy, Charles, 49
Perlman, Herbert L., 51
Phillips, J. Donald, 41, 42, 44, 47–48, 52
Potomac Company, 15

Q

Qianlong, Emperor, 73–74

R

Reagan, Ronald, 25, 26, 51
Republican Party, 24, 26
Revolutionary War. *See* American Revolution
Roche, George C., 48, 49, 50n1, 51–52

S

Sheridan, Philip, 36
Sixth Circuit Court of Appeals, 51
Socrates, 54
Souvenir, 27

Spring Arbor, Michigan, 19, 20
Sprague Committee, 41n1
Sputnik, 41–42, 43
State of the Union address, 14
Student Federal Loan Program, 43. *See also* National Defense Student Loan, National Direct Student Loan
Supreme Court, 43–44

T

Tao, 67
Tangerine Bowl (1955), 42
Tatel, David S., 50,
Thomas, Clarence, 98
Title IX, 48, 49, 51
Treptow, Martin, 25

U

United States Code, 2
University of Michigan, 20, 56, 57
University of Virginia Law School, 68

V

Veterans Benefits, 48, 49

W

Washington, George, 4, 8, 13–15, 16, 25
Waters, Muddy, 42
Weightman, Roger, 11
West Point, 14
White, Andrew Dickson, 35–37, 38, 39, 73
Wilson, Woodrow, 34